T0347661

Parkflyer

Parkflyer

Hinrik Schulte

Special Interest Model Books

Special Interest Model Books Ltd.
P.O.Box 327
Poole
Dorset
BH15 2RG
England

First published by Verlag fur Technik und Handwerk 2002

This English edition published by Special Interest Model Books Ltd. 2005

ISBN 1-85486-236-7

www.specialinterestmodelbooks.co.uk

Printed in Malta by Interprint Limited

CONTENTS

INTRODUCTION

Model Flying – Whenever You Like

Model flying on a quiet evening in the middle of the week sounds great! But, as always, the time schedule is tight and there is barely enough time to drive to the flying field, and rig up a big and complicated model aircraft before the light goes. This is the moment, when you wish you have a small and uncomplicated aircraft, that could be flown in the garden or on the football field without great effort. Your spare time would just be enough for this type of flying.

The first "Park Flyers" surely thought more or less the same way and started building and flying such models. The aircraft were simple and uncomplicated and their flying properties enabled them to fly in limited spaces without bothering other users.

At that time they could barely foresee, that this simple but logical idea would become so popular, that it would be the start of a new model category. Only a few people started the movement, but now, a few years later, even the modelling industry has picked up the trend.

It is typical that the big model firms join these trends very late on and the movement was initially serviced by a "cottage industry", offering planes, kits as well as motors, gearboxes and batteries. Nevertheless today we are able to find all the accessories mentioned in a good model shop just round the corner.

Even sceptical modellers can't fully ignore the trend and today almost every modeller owns a Parkflyer for a snatched flight between two appointments.

Flying a Parkflyer does not demand too much with regards to site and the modern Parkflyer can also stand a bit of wind, so that there are amazingly many opportunities to use these light models for two or three flights "just in-between".

All the above thoughts apply to the writer the same way. Just have such a small plane ready for take-off in your hobby room and you will be able to practice your hobby for relaxation after work and before the family takes over. When flying Parkflyers, you will soon find that they are not only good for beginners. Sure enough, most Parkflyers are suitable for inexperienced pilots, but even the modellers with long experience, and with about 25 years of electric model flying (I would count myself in this group), will soon find out, that it is a lot of fun to fly around trees, hedges and street lamps. Smooth flying at walking pace provides a lot of fun for those people who normally only fly with full throttle. They won't believe it at first, but once infected, they won't be able to fight the disease any more.

The pleasure of model flying really comes first with these small aircraft and it is really more fun to fly a Parkflyer than you can imagine before having tried; you can become addicted.

Apart from that, Parkflyers have changed in their development, the power train especially has improved very much in the last years. Parkflyers are no longer systematically under powered and needing full throttle to maintain level flight or for a slow climb. Modern Parkflyers have powerful motors and batteries and are able to perform aerobatics with no problem.

Even from the point of view of cost, Parkflyers have reached a very affordable price level. Basically everything you need is produced in large quantities and the prices for servos, receivers as well as all the other components are on a normal level. The lightweight receivers today are cheaper than the "normal" ones and the small servos are also only slightly higher in price than the cheap "standard" servos. Batteries, motors and controllers are even cheaper than for most of the other electric models. At the end of the day, a Parkflyer is usually cheaper than even a simple glider with electric motor. This has been different before, but the trend towards the Parkflyer has caused this reduction in price, although some modellers have not yet noticed it.

In the course of many "park flights" with a lot of different models, I have been able to tailor significantly different flight characteristics of my models to suit them to different flying sites.

I would like to analyse these differences and give explanations that will help the newcomer in this field of model flying to select the right plane and equipment for his requirements. I hope too that it will attract the attention of further modellers to this interesting way of model flying.

But this book has not only been written to educate; entertainment is also one of the targets and I hope you won't find it boring to get informed. I can promise you will find park flying much more interesting than expected once you have started flying your own Parkflyer.

Hinrik Schulte 2005

CHAPTER ONE

Models and Flying – Some Basics

How do we define a Parkflyer?

You won't find any definition of a Parkflyer that is totally comprehensive within this book as even the author finds it hard to settle on a complete definition.

There is no doubt, that a Parkflyer is bigger, heavier and also faster flying than a true slow flyer which is designed to fly in a gym or, only with absolutely calm conditions, outside, but even here the borderline is unclear. With a lightweight and slow Parkflyer you can also fly indoors and there are quite a few Models that are suitable for outdoor flying as well as for indoor flying.

Finding the borderline between a Parkflyer and a "normal" electric flyer is even harder. Should 600grams be the weight limit, or 800grams? And we can even find or build

The Ikarus Bleriot was one of the first Parkflyers on the market. Subsequently models have gone through a long development curve.

With a 90 cm Wingspan and 500 grams of weight, the Graupner biplane Sunwheel is a fully grown model aircraft, but nevertheless the Sunwheel has very good Parkflyer properties.

models weighing 1000grams that can be flown like other Parkflyers. There is definitely no clear borderline.

It is also impossible to use wingspan as the dividing criterion. A Speed 400 pylon racer is definitely within the weight limit and the wingspan of 70 to 80cm equates to a Parkflyer - nevertheless, the pylon racer is not a Parkflyer at all.

Having said before, the difference to a slow flyer is not big either and you can use many Parkflyers in a big gym, as long as the wing loading is low enough. So they are big Slowflyers as much as light Parkflyers. Very light models will not bring so much pleasure to the Pilot outdoors and should be flown indoors. If we are in an urgent need of a definition, we could probably use the wing

loading as a distinguishing factor. A slow flyer for indoor use requires a wing loading around 10g/sq.dm, while a Parkflyer can stand more and definitely needs more, if you want to fly in windy conditions too.

I propose to define a Parkflyer by the way you want to use the plane. A Parkflyer should be designed in a way, that you can safely launch, fly and land the model in places that are not definitely designed as a model flying field. A school playing field, a supermarket car park or the local park can provide a suitable space to fly and land the model in a safe and controlled way. You can surely do this with a lot of different planes, but you will also soon find out, that there are planes that you feel comfortable flying in these locations and others you don't really want to fly outside a model field because it is getting stressful. Those latter are definitely not Parkflyers!

With the right model, park flying is easy and relaxing and a true pleasure for the Pilot. The model should have a high manoeuvrability and it must be able to fly safely at low speeds. Apart from that, it must not require a long glide path for landing. An open space of 30-50 metres, maybe a small football field, will be enough to perform a full flight schedule as well as a controlled landing. The landing strip as such, probably does not need to be that big, but you also need room to set up the final approach.

Apart from that, the model must not emit too much noise to avoid trouble with the neighbours. This normally excludes glow or diesel engine powered planes, even with effective silencers and limits us to electric propulsion. But even so, we have some bad examples of loud electric models. You won't believe how much noise you can produce even with a small Speed 280 motor.

When are put all these requirements together, the definition of a Parkflyer is not complete, but we can put together some technical data, that will apply to most of the Parkflyers around:

Wingspan: between 80-120cm
Take-off weight: between 200-800 grams
Wing loading: between 10-25 g/sq.dm
Electric powered
Fully working landing gear (maybe a glider with folding propeller can live without it)

This list is not complete, but we will see that most Parkflyers somehow fit into the framework given, if they are going to be able to fly as mentioned above.

Which model aircraft are suitable for park flying?

Simply, all those planes that fulfil the above requirements! But this answer is a bit too easy. Otherwise you could just take that list and quit reading. If your Parkflyer is to be somehow scale-like, you should take a look at the aircraft designed at the beginning of manned flying. They were designed to fly with little motor power and a low wing loading. For the same reason, we can also look at modern ultra-light planes. Nevertheless, in most cases you won't be able to get away without increasing the chord of the wing in order to get more wing surface and a low load.

If you are not looking at original planes at all, you have got the freedom to design your plane according to your need and create as much wing area as you want or need to achieve the wing loading that is desired. The wing loading of a Parkflyer is always the crucial point, it will later have a big influence on the flying speed and manoeuvrability of the Parkflyer as well as on the landing characteristics.

Contrary to other model aircraft, good glide performance is not really desired for a Parkflyer because this would increase the required area for the approach and landing and make landing in difficult locations harder. Another reason why many Parkflyers have flat plate wing sections. For the same reason, only few Parkflyers are pure gliders. They are too good for the park, seen from the aerodynamic point of view. The scene is rather dominated by light, but carefully motorised model aircraft with electric power. For these powered aircraft we also need suitable landing gear, that protects the fuselage while landing on paved ground. For noise reasons, we can eliminate IC powered models.

As to the point of construction of a Parkflyer, we shall see later, that we are free to use many different methods and materials, as long as the weight of the constructions stays within the given limits. Light building, must be the first and most important rule anyway and a small pair of scales should always be present while building or completing a Parkflyer. No matter whether it is wood, Styrofoam, Depron, carbon fibre or glass fibre. Everything is possible, if you want to build your own Parkflyer, but in many cases only the careful combination of different materials results in a really lightweight Parkflyer.

The commercial marketplace currently offers a wide variety of model constructional methods and materials to the modeller. Of course the modeller also has the opportunity to design his own Parkflyer; there are few secrets to building light models and it is possible to find enough ideas and suggestions in the usual magazines and books that can be applied to Parkflyers. In most cases the plans offered are not even very complicated and even an inexperienced modeller will be able 'to complete his own Parkflyer built from scratch.

Where can I fly with my Parkflyer?

This is of course the next question that comes into mind, when we are thinking about the acquisition of a Parkflyer. Either we need to find a suitable site for the chosen model or, if a potential site is available, make sure the model is suitable for the site. First of all, we should point out, that it is not forbidden to use a Parkflyer on the local model flying field; usually just the opposite! This would be the ideal place with a lot of free space for flying and landing and only limited spectators and neighbours that won't cause any trouble. Please do not underestimate this advantage, especially for the initial flight of a new model that is not so familiar to you that you want to fly under difficult circumstances. So, maybe you should test your Parkflyer on the model flying field first and get used to the plane and its habits before you fly in a challenging location such as your own garden or the street in front of the house.

By the way, flying in your own garden sitting on the terrace is a dream, isn't it? No long drive to the flying field, you won't be away from the family too long, a lot of comfort, and the supply of cold drinks is guaranteed. Unfortunately most of use just live in the wrong location to make this dream come true as the garden is too small or there is not enough free space for a proper landing approach. Free space is the keyword. Houses, garages, trees, bushes and fences will make park flying hard. You should really have a lot of room or know your model very well to try these stunts.

I can at least say, that my garden is definitely too small with a 120cm high hedge to fly over and still land on the grass safely. Furthermore there is a small, but prominent tree limiting the landing path to a width of about 3 metres, and that's just before you smash into the greenhouse! Therefore I was very pleased to see that the local school were building a nice parking area for busses just 100 metres away from my house. This parking lot has dimensions of about 60x60 metres, is fully paved and there are no houses next to it in at least three directions. Even the bushes around the bus park that are now about 2 metres high are no real problem due to the size of the space. Just a shame, that there are some lamp posts right in the middle. But maybe they are obstacles, maybe they are challenges. We will come to that point later.

It is not only the location that can make the place an ideal spot for Parkflyers. It is also the fact, that the place won't be used in the evening and during the weekends. Apart from that, the closest neighbour is the author himself, so there are no complaints about noise to be expected. Even a little wind, doesn't do any harm, as you can start directly into the wind in most cases without too much turbulence. We shall see how this develops when the bushes and trees grow higher. But again, you can see this problem as a challenge too.

Unfortunately there are not too many places as ideal as this, but if you drive through

This scratch built Depron Parkflyer is suitable for Indoor flying as well as Parkflying.

your neighbourhood with open (park flyer's) eyes, you will surely find a few locations that are similar to the description above. Furthermore most villages or small communities as well as most schools have a football field which is more than good enough for park flying too. Apart from the regular training and playing times there should be room for model flying too and one thing is for sure, we do not do any harm to the grass when flying over it.

Even normal schoolyards are often big enough for a Parkflyer. The only disadvantage is the fact, the most of the time buildings are very close and you will find turbulence even in light wind conditions. This can turn flying of a 300gram model into a real challenge.

The car parks of supermarkets and Shopping Malls could also be a good idea, as long as you find times, when they are closed. It's worth a try anyway. Furthermore you will find street and parking areas in industrial estates that are barely used over the weekend and offer enough room for park flying. Here

again you should check out the places carefully, maybe even a cul-de-sac can turn into a runway, but please take heed of the security advice below.

The same applies to small tracks in the fields of farmland. Even a narrow road is enough to serve as a runway for take-off and landing and all the other flying will happen over the fields anyway. As long as the track follows the wind direction more or less it is a great challenge and if you can bring your Parkflyer down there safely, you can fly anywhere.

Please be careful using private ground as a flying field, you will have to respect the obvious rights of the owner. We will come to this point talking about legal aspects in future pages.

So, we better go back to the public open spaces and up to now we have missed out the obvious! For good reason, we borrowed the name for our planes from the public parks. This is where it all started and if you live in a bigger city, model flying used to be a problem because you had to

The author's son Felix with Elfi.

drive long distances to be able to fly your model. But with the right model, flying in a public park is no problem at all, as long as the area is big enough.

Selecting the right location

We cannot leave aside the point of noise. A well-selected powertrain is quiet, but never 100% noiseless. For this reason the neighbours of suitable locations may feel disturbed from time to time. In order to avoid trouble from the beginning, we should respect their feelings and refrain from flying late in the evening. Rude behaviour does a lot of harm to our hobby in general.

Just to make the list complete, we can come back to flying Parkflyers indoors. Provided the hall is big enough and the plane has a high degree of manoeuvrability, this is not a problem. But you must not forget that a wrong estimation of your flying skills might lead to harsh punishment. Walls, ceilings and other obstacle are absolutely unwilling to jump aside, when a model aircraft comes too close. Believe me, I have experience of this!

Safety first!

Up until now, I have written about suitable locations for park flying, but there are definitely some points, that will turn a possible area into one which we cannot fly at all. Here are some points, that should be considered before takeoff.

First of all, please keep your brain switched on! There are so many possible locations, that you will always be able to find a good one and there is no need to make half-hearted compromises or to insist on flying even when you bother the neighbours or cause danger to them.

You should only fly near motorways or streets with heavy traffic, when you can be absolutely sure, that the model will not go down there, even when it is out of control. The consequences of a traffic accident, caused by a model aircraft out of control, could be enormous and we should avoid that danger right from the start.

High voltage power lines are another dangerous point. Not only for the model

Parkflying is not only a hobby for summer, equipped with simple skis the Robbe Stieglitz provides continuing fun even in the winter.

aircraft, probably also for the person that wants to recover a plane stranded in such a power line.

For an experienced modeller it is clear, that he will not fly his model near a model flying field, at least not before the question of frequencies has been checked. Another risk, especially in park flying is the fact, that a flying model soon attracts the attention of passers-by, when you fly in public areas the Pilot is quickly surrounded by interested spectators. This is good and perfect publicity for our hobby, but especially in these situations, the Pilot has a high responsibility. Please do not let yourself be lead into risky manoeuvres, just because the audience wants see them. Concentrate 100% on your model and avoid any risk right from the beginning. In such cases it is useful to have a second person with you to watch the scene and answer questions, so that the Pilot can focus on his flying.

Another risk in park flying is the lack of care that can occur when you operate a Parkflyer. True enough, flying a small and lightweight model is less dangerous than flying a 20Kg model with a large motor. Nevertheless a small model aircraft can also do a lot of harm to persons and objects. Once again, please keep your brain switched on. Other model Pilots can be very dangerous landmarks, because in most cases they also carry a transmitter sending out radio signals. If you come too close with your model to the other Pilot's transmitter, it is highly possible, that he will disturb your receiver, if his signal is stronger than yours. Suddenly you might be in trouble controlling your model, even if you never had problems before. This way you might loose control over your model and you are lucky, if only the plane gets damaged.

You should not be careless in building and servicing your Parkflyer. It is logical, that we

A scratch-built Suchoj aerobatic flyer. The wing has a conventional section but the fuselage is only a profile.

should only be flying models that are fully checked and operated to the highest standards. The primary reason for this care is the wish to avoid a crash with the model that might damage or destroy it. But many Pilots neglect their Parkflyers thinking that the damage caused by a crash with such a light model will not be all that serious. Of course this way of thinking is absolutely wrong. A Parkflyer out of control can cause as much damage as most other models. Whenever you are in doubt, please do not fly your model before the problem is fixed.

Nothing new, most readers will think up to now. You are right; as long as you maintain the same standards of safety flying a Parkflyer as if you were flying a big, and expensive model, nothing serious will happen and park flying is real fun!

Some considerations whilst flying Parkflyers

Of course, a Parkflyer in general is nothing else but a "normal" model aircraft controlled via two or three axes, but there are still some details you should keep in mind.

Once you have looked into the matter more closely and have checked the situations for which Parkflyers have been designed, you will first of all find out, that a Parkflyer is not the ideal beginner's model, even if it looks very much like that.

Flying in confined spaces needs a lot of concentration, especially if a flying altitude of 10 metres is already regarded as a safe flying level and the same applies when obstacles in the flight path are rather the rule than the exception.

The low weight of the models, generally between 300 and 600g and the low wing loadings are generally positive flying attributes, but they are also responsible for the fact, that flying a Parkflyer is often heavily affected by wind. If the wing loading is under 20g/dm.sq, even light winds make it difficult to control the plane and suddenly the wind has more

The first Parkflyer glider on the market. This little Lo 100 really is a sweetheart.

influence on the plane than the commands of the Pilot.

In judging the wind, you should not only rely on weather reports, but safety often depends on the exact situation at the location. This again applies most frequently, when you are flying in confined spaces. Depending on the exact direction of the wind, a row of trees or a building can either be the perfect windshield in windy conditions and you can fly there when the wind strength would not normally allow. Whereas, in other places they can cause turbulence, even in light winds, that make flying nearly impossible because the light aircraft will dance like autumn leaves in the wind.

The model flying field of the author is a good example of this effect. On the south side of the flying field I have a forest with 20 metre high trees. If the wind comes from the south, the place is totally calm up to a height of about 20 metres and up to a distance of about 50 metres from the trees. There you can fly the lightest slow flyer even in windy conditions, but if you leave this area, even a 2Kg IC powered sports model goes up and down by 5 metres a second and a Parkflyer is smashed into the ground easily.

But on such a day with southern winds, you have a lot of room to fly a Parkflyer in the calm zone, and it is more fun than any other model. If the wind comes from other directions, it depends on the wind speed, but on a calm day it is also a lot of fun to fly there and the 80 x 40 metres are more than sufficient to have a lot of fun without leaving the airfield at all.

As most of the Parkflyers have undercambered wing profiles, they have a big problem fighting winds. Models with conventionally profiled wings have a clear advantage in these circumstance and they also have a flatter glidepath.

Planes with a curved plate as wing profile

generally need a lower flying speed and do not stall that easily, but they always need a bit of power from the motor to stay up. Especially when it comes to landing, you should keep that in mind. Once the speed controller has switched off the power supply for the motor at 2 metres height, you will see that the Parkflyer has a strong desire to return to terra firma. You are lucky if the ground is suitable for a landing.

In order to avoid the, sometimes painful, experience you should keep an eye on the flight time and the voltage level of your battery and you should rather land a little bit earlier than waiting for the speed controller to switch off. This is harder, when you are flying with reduced rpm's for most of the time. With reduced throttle you can barely hear the battery fading and you might get a surprise. In this case it helps to open the throttle fully for a short moment from time to time to check the battery status. In this situation you would also be grateful to have a speed controller indicating the battery level, for example by changing the motor voltage up and down a bit before switching off.

Due to the bad gliding properties of most Parkflyers, it is advisable to land with the motor on at low rpm. A well-trimmed Parkflyer can be landed with the throttle stick only, not touching the elevator at all. Landings without power are normally not all that good, unless you want to check out your landing gear.

In any case you work more with the throttle stick in a Parkflyer than in most other model categories. Flying a motorised glider, the motor is only used at full power to climb and in many other models the throttle is only used digitally. Full power – no power. When flying Parkflyers often only one click more on the throttle is enough to make the model climb, fly level or sink at the rate that is required at that moment. Part of the fun in park flying to use the elevator only in order to stabilise the model when turning. Changes of the flying altitude can only be made with the motor. This should be practised, because it is very important for flying in confined areas. If you do not move the throttle carefully here, the model soon builds up too much speed and the flying space seems to reduce in size very quickly. Full throttle either means a steep climb or a "relatively" high speed and both things will lead to a stressful situation very quickly. Practice is the only thing that helps.

Luckily enough modern electronic speed controllers (ESC's) are designed to handle long periods of reduced speed without any problem and the possibility to control the motor speed precisely increases the fun in flying significantly.

Once you're not flying alone any more, it is advisable, that the Pilots stay together in a small area. Due to the generally close distance between the transmitter and the model you could otherwise come into a situation, where the other Pilot's transmitter is closer to your model, than your own and his signal might cause a disturbance to your model. Modern receivers should be able to cope with this, but there can be moments of lost control that might turn into a serious problem at 2 metre flight level.

These short safety and flying advise notes show, that even a Parkflyer demands a certain level of care and responsibility from the Pilot. Unlike many other models, a Parkflyer is not normally flown in the middle of wide open spaces where the plane cannot cause any serious damage to third parties or objects when it gets out of control.

A Parkflyer is destined to fly in areas where leaving the normal flying sector can lead to a lot of complications for the Pilot as well as for others. You should keep this in mind all the time.

Legal aspects

First of all, we should point out, that the author strongly believes that no hobby is worth a meeting in front of a law court. We should keep this in mind, if we are looking into the legal aspects of model flying in this chapter.

In order to maintain a good image of model flying by the public it makes sense to fly a model aircraft only in those places where we do not limit the personal freedom of third parties or bother other people at all. So, if one of your fellow citizens feels disturbed by a model aircraft, please refrain from taking this as an opportunity to prove that you have the right to fly in this special place at this special time. It is, as always, advisable to seek a compromise and come to a solution that is acceptable for all parties. In every case it is better to try and see the matter from both sides rather than starting serious conflicts if you could also fly in a different place, or maybe at a different time.

But of course, model Pilots have certain rights too, but do we need to insist on them all of the time?

We should also point out the author is not a lawyer at all and experience is the primary source of his knowledge in these points. Therefore he cannot accept any liability for the complete correctness of the statements below in every special case.

Obviously we won't find any laws or paragraphs that are specially dedicated to Parkflyers, but we can apply the same basics as for any other model aircraft. The only difference lies in the point, that we are not talking about flying on a dedicated site for model aircraft but we are looking at the aspects of flying in a public park or in populated areas and here we have slightly different rules sometimes.

Where am I allowed to fly?

This basic question has to be divided in two aspects. One part is starting and landing the model aircraft and where the Pilot stands and the other part is the ground below our flight path.

The second part is quite obvious, because you are generally allowed to fly over any location, even without the acceptance of the owner. Otherwise British Airways or the RAF would also need a permit to fly over private ground from each and every owner. So, the airspace over your neighbour's garden is generally free. There are obvious exceptions to this rule, but it is in our own interest, not to fly in the approach zone of the local airport anyway, isn't it?

The question of starting and landing is clearly more difficult. Of course you may use your own ground as well as public ground, like streets, parks or public sports fields to start and land your Parkflyer. Things are getting serious when we come to private property of third parties. Here the owner or an authorised person clearly has the right to expel you from the private ground. Even more so, when the private ground is protected by a wall or fence. Crossing this protection is clearly called trespass. Therefore we should forget about these sites for flying.

But what happens, if the Parkflyer touches ground in such a fenced area when landing or when it crashes? Most important, the owner of the land can only retain the remains of the model in order to identify the damage that has been caused and the identity of the owner of the model aircraft. After these points have been settled, he has to return the model. Clear enough: When a model aircraft, this applies to all kinds of models, comes down in your neighbour's garden, you should ask him for permission to recover the plane and he has no reason to refuse. If the plane has crashed into the bonnet of his new car leaving damage, he has got the right to hold the model back until he has taken all means to secure the proof that the damage has been caused by the model aircraft, if necessary, by the local police. In worst case he can hold back the model until the full name and address of the model owner or the Pilot has been established. After that, he has got no reason to refuse the return of the aircraft. Please keep in mind, if your model regularly lands in your neighbour's garden killing roses and other valuables, your own garden is either too small or your flying skills are insufficient for this location.

Does a passer-by in the park have the right to forbid flying for example? First of all, no. A model Pilot has the same rights as anybody else to follow his hobbies in the park providing that no local bye-laws exist to prohibit him. But please, do not switch off your brains after this sentence and insist on your position at any cost. Probably we should first of all try to understand the other person and find out, why he thinks that model flying is so disturbing in this place. Often we are only talking about little details and a bit of discussion can solve the problem. If there is no possibility of finding a compromise though, there is no reason to step back by any means. Only the police or specially authorised officials should have the right to expel a model flyer from public grounds, but in case one of these institutions insists, we should not start any long discussions any more but stop flying.

The discussion becomes more difficult when the question of whether model flying is bothering or disturbing in general is raised. The definition of "disturbance" is so wide, that we can only try to argue on an unemotional basis about these things. It often helps to explain the model to the opponent and show him, that such a tiny and light structure surely is no danger to his health or life. But after that, please refrain from strafing the next park bench.

The bottom line is always the same. Please carry on using your common sense and try to understand the other person too. At any time, we are also talking about the reputation of our hobby, model flying with the public. A block-headed model Pilot, and there are a few, can be the reason that model flying is banned totally from a park or a football field and this does great harm to all of us.

Well insured

The insurance aspect of park flying is again the same as for any other model aircraft. All the general aspects and rules for the operation of model aircraft apply to Parkflyers as well as to other model aircraft and the conditions of their insurance are all the same.

There is no legal obligation to have a public liability insurance at all. It is advisable for every model Pilot to have a special liability insurance for model aircraft. This must expressly cover model flying outside dedicated model flying fields to be useful to a Parkflyer Pilot. Those insurances are offered by the model flyers associations such as the British Model Flying Association (BMFA) via their affiliated clubs or on a "lone wolf" basis at an affordable price.

In my personal opinion, model flying without a public liability insurance, even if there is no legal obligation to have one, is irresponsible. Even minor damage, like a broken mirror on a car, can easily cost something like £150, this equals the insurance premium of the next ten years easily.

At the end of this chapter, the author has to point out once again, even if it is the third time, that we must use our common sense at all times. This applies as much to the point of a public liability insurance as also to the modeller's behaviour towards the public when flying a Parkflyer in the face of opposition.

Insisting on our own position is never the way forward. This will only lead our fellow citizens to insist on their own positions too and that won't take us anywhere. So better refrain from flying over our neighbours terrace, when he is taking a nap on an early Sunday afternoon and rather take a round of flying in the early evening, when he is not disturbed any more. A compromise can always be found, if both parties are willing to move.

CHAPTER TWO

Construction Methods for Parkflyers

In general it can be stated, that any known construction method for Model aircraft can be used for the construction of a Parkflyer, as long as it results in a lightweight model. Building light is the beginning and the end for every Parkflyer, by the way, for every model aircraft. Finally the flying habits of a Parkflyer strongly depend on the weight of the model. Only a lightweight model can fly slowly and can turn with small radius and these are the properties our Parkflyers desperately need. Once it's guaranteed that the model will have the right, i.e. *light,* weight, the correct construction method is only a matter of selection of the right method for the planned model. A real "old timer" would probably be built from balsa and spruce than from carbon or Styrofoam. On the other hand, the model of a modern aircraft may be build from modern materials too.

Looking at the different construction methods in every detail is enough for at least one completely new book. Therefore we will only take a brief look at the most popular construction methods and try to point out some specialities of the different methods and their preferable application.

Wooden construction

Thinking about lightweight model aircraft, most thoughts will still go in the direction of balsawood, that classical material for model aircraft for many years. As is so often the case, first thoughts are absolutely correct! Balsawood is definitely a good material for the construction of light model aircraft, if you know how to use it and if you know a few little tricks for the reinforcement of balsa planes.

As a matter of fact, the first Slowflyers, the light brothers and sisters of our Parkflyers, were build from balsa strip and sheet only and they had excellent flying properties. In the meantime the market offers a wide selection of wooden models where all the parts are precisely cut by CNC controlled milling machines and laser and water jet cutters. These kits have perfectly fitting parts and result in wonderful wooden constructions with a perfect finish and are astonishingly strong.

Another early Parkflyer. The Simprop Taube is of completely wooden construction covered with heat-shrink film. A bit of nostalgia.

But by building with wood you are not dependent on kits only. Wood is also a perfect material to build a Parkflyer from scratch according to your own ideas.

With the help of balsa strips it is easy to design a light and strong fuselage that can be left open or be covered with paper or heat shrink covering. Especially for models of aircraft from the beginning of flying, wooden construction is more or less a must. The original was built the same way.

Balsa strip can either be bought in the local model shop, or you can produce your own from sheet balsa with the help of a simple stripping tool. This can save a lot of money

on one hand and on the other hand you are also able to easily produce just the right size of balsa strip for your model. The right dimension of the balsa strips is the secret to building light, but first of all, we have to select the right sheet of balsa for cutting the strips. Very light and soft balsa is good for filling blocks, but not for strips. For this, a medium hard sheet of balsa is far more suitable otherwise we have to work with very thick material and that's not elegant at all. Apart from that, a few reinforcements with spruce strips won't do any harm if they are used carefully. The front part of the fuselage of a model should be relatively strong, as the heavy motor is installed there and it is always the nose that touches ground first, if the landing is not all that perfect. As a compensation, the rear section of the fuselage, behind the trailing edge of the wings, can be designed very light. The forces this part of the body has to withstand are much lower than normally expected.

The formers of the fuselage can also be made from balsa strips. Four strips of 3x10mm balsa glued together with overlapping corners will have the right grain direction of the wood in all directions and make a very strong former with double wall thickness in the corners, where the main stringers are glued to the former. Furthermore, we need special strength where the battery sits in the fuselage and at the assembly points of the wings and at the

landing gear attachment point.

When building a Parkflyer from wood, it is also important to use the right glue. Too much white glue or 5 Minute Epxoy will add too much weight to the construction and will harm the flying properties of the finished model. Thin cyanoacrylate (Superglue) is just right for balsa as it guarantees good joint at low weight. White glue does not have any advantages at all and 5 Minute Epoxy should only be used carefully in places where wood and metal have to be glued together.

Naturally the spars of the wings have to carry most of the load, but the load is reducing from the middle to the wingtips and therefore the size of the spar can also be reduced continuously on the way to the wingtips. The ribs of the wings can be made from 1.5mm balsa, the spars should be, depending on the

A complete material mix. The sides of the fuselage are from Depron, reinforced with balsa strips and a former from balsa with aluminium tubes for the fuselage.

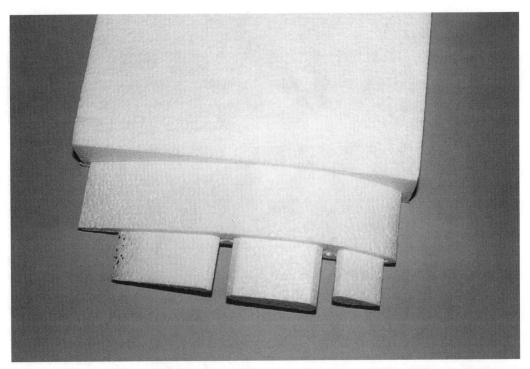

The work of a professional Styrofoam cutter. The core of this wing is hollowed to reduce weight.

final weight of the plane, made from spruce.

If the wings are not completely sheeted with balsa, they will need to be covered. Here we also have a number of alternatives. The lightest method would probably be tissue covering, but in most cases the necessary painting will possibly warp the light balsa structure and make the wing unusable. Much better are heat shrink films that only shrink a small amount, for example Ecospan from Graupner. Ecospan is also very light, because it is not coated with glue. The glue has to be painted onto the wood before covering and therefore there is only glue in the places, where it is actually needed.

Apart from that, Ecospan has a slightly rough surface that causes a turbulent airflow over the wings which has a positive effect on the minimum speed of our Parkflyer.

Transparent Oracover Light also has a very light weight and is suitable for a Parkflyer

that is designed to fly a little faster. The smooth surface is very good for gliders, and it is often used for hand launched soarers.

Parkflyers from Styrofoam

There is a definite trend in direction for Parkflyers made more or less entirely from Styrofoam that cannot be ignored. Multiplex, especially, has set the standards with models like Smiley, Twinstar, Teddy and also the Pico Cub.

The parts for these models, the fuselage, the wings and the tail feather, are formed in a mould, just like those Styrofoam parts that protect a new DVD Player during transportation. Apart from an expensive mould quite big machines are needed for the moulding process. These are normally not available to a modeller.

Nevertheless we can use the material Styrofoam also for our own designs. For many

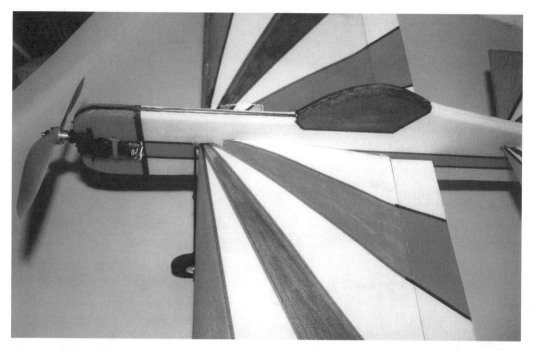

Once again the Silhouette Suchoj. The carbon rod reinforcing the fuselage is clearly visible in the front section.

years the wings of model aircraft have been made from Styrofoam cores that have been cut with a hot wire from a block. These wing cores are of course also very well suited to Parkflyers. We don't even have to sheet them with balsa or obeche. Some balsa strips, inserted as spars will give these wings sufficient stability for a Parkflyer. The rough surface of the Styrofoam does not require any treatment, except for some colouring, if demanded. As mentioned before, a smooth surface is not an advantage, if you want to fly at low speed and if you finish such a model with just a bit of foam-friendly spray paint or an Edding pen, the rough surface is barely visible.

If a smooth surface is required, the Styrofoam can also be sanded with 400 grain abrasive paper and later be treated with a thin layer of filler. This way even a Styrofoam wing can have a very even surface, but be careful with the weight of the filler. Deluxe Materials "Modellite" is an ideal filler for the purpose.

Otherwise, Roofmate, the blue foam is also a very good material, but it is much heavier than Styrofoam and we must keep a very close eye on the weight here.

Working with Styrofoam, it is mandatory to keep the weight of glues and paint under control. Only places that require a high strength should be glued with 5 Minute Epoxy. Small spots can be glued with foam friendly cyano and bigger areas like sheeting can be glued with spray contact glue.

The professionals are also able to cut the fuselages of their model from Styrofoam blocks, but this is far more complicated than producing wings, especially if the fuselages need to be hollowed to reduce weight. This requires a CNC controlled cutting machine or a lot of experience.

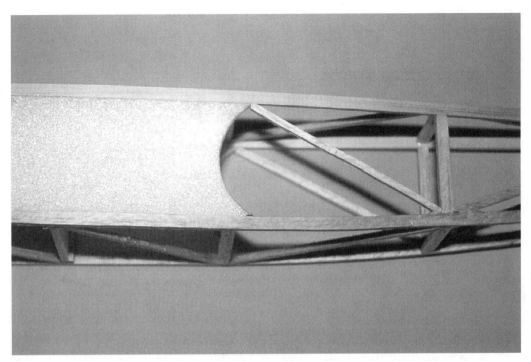

The combination of Depron and balsa strips makes the model light and strong.

Parkflyers from Depron

Many readers may think that Depron is the same as Styrofoam and they are not absolutely wrong. In some respects these two materials have a few things in common, yet their handling is totally different.

Depron can be found in the hobby and garden market where it is sold as an insulation layer that is used to line walls under wall paper. It is sold in sheets of 3 or 6 mm thickness. Depron has a white surface and can be cut easily with a sharp Stanley knife. It is quite simple to design complete Parkflyers from Depron sheet; wings as well as fuselages. The material cost of a Parkflyer designed from Depron is less than £5 and so many modellers are tempted to use the material for a lot of experiments, that cost close to nothing, even if the experiment fails.

The white surface of Depron can again be coloured with suitable paints, even if we will never manage to achieve a glossy finish. A special point has to be made concerning the word "suitable" because Depron as well as Styrofoam is not resistant to many solvents and most colour paints will destroy Depron.

The same applies to the glue. Normal cyano or UHU Hart will attack the structure of Depron and destroy it. Suitable glues are again white glue, foam-friendly cyano, UHU-Por and epoxy for special points. At this point the author has to admit his special affection for foam-friendly cyano. This glue will normally need about 10 minutes to dry on Depron, but with the help of, again a foam friendly, activator, you can work in seconds. This is especially welcome, when it comes to repair jobs in the field. Finding the right activator is unfortunately a matter of trial and error.

Another easy way of giving colour to a Depron is a design using Edding markers.

This is all that is necessary to colour the Sukhoi.

With the help of some pens in different colours and a ruler astonishing effects are possible.

Unfortunately Depron in itself is not very strong and especially wings made from it won't last without reinforcements from either balsa wood, spruce or - even better from carbon rods.

But Depron is not only a good material for own designs, even the model industry has found out about the properties of this material and is using it more and more. Presently we see a large number of kits and ARTF's (Almost Ready to Fly) made from Depron filling the market place.

Here the makers of the models again use a technique derived from the packing industry. The parts for the models are vacuum formed under the influence of temperature. This way it is possible to produce even complicated fuselages and complete wings with "real" profiles. Together with industrial methods of sealing the surface, the models can even be sold with a complete finish that pleases the customer. Some innovative companies are busy developing more and more sophisticated techniques to produce Depron Models that are way beyond our imagination. This development is only in the early stages today and we will surely see more and bigger model aircraft made from vacuum formed Depron in the near future in our model shops.

Further construction methods

The above mentioned construction methods are used for the majority of Parkflyers that can be seen in the field, yet there are also other ways to build a Parkflyer that have proven to be successful for building light models, although they are not widely used.

Building Fuselages from glass fibre reinforced plastic (GRP) is one of these

30

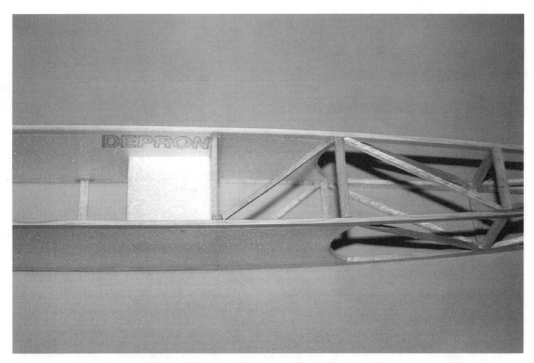

Depron is an ideal material for the construction of Parkflyers.

techniques which is rarely used, although it is possible, to build a light fuselage this way. If the fuselage is designed for the use in a light model from the beginning, there will only be the minimum of reinforcement to keep the weight low. This also means on the other hand, that the final part will probably give the impression, that it is very fragile and the sides of the fuselage seem weak, but only this way it is possible to keep the weight within limits.

Another technique is building a model from carbon Rods only. This is the basis of very light models, mostly Slowflyers for indoor applications. These models are quite exclusive because of their low weight but the construction is also very strong due to the fact, that the carbon rods, especially if they are bent, can absorb a lot of energy in the event of a bad landing. More and more, carbon rods and carbon tubes are playing a big role in building Parkflyers as reinforcing elements,

giving light structures the right strength.

Finally it must be mentioned, that many successful designs are based on a mix of different construction techniques. A wooden fuselage with a wing made of Depron, or a fuselage with Depron formers and balsa sheeting or strips or with carbon rods for the stability are good examples for successful combinations of different materials.

Here we have endless possibilities and not all of them have been tested so far. Nevertheless we will find some of them later in this book, looking at the individual models.

Equipment for the workshop

One advantage of Parkflyers, that should not be underestimated, is the fact, that we are talking about relatively simple models and the assembly of these models does not require too much equipment.

Many kits for Parkflyers as designed and

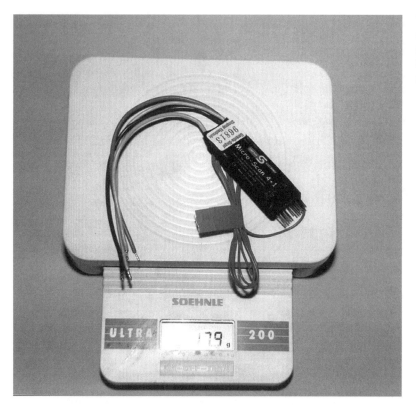

The most important aid to constructing an own-design Parkflyer is an accurate scale.

prepared in a way, that makes it easy and clean to assemble the model in the kitchen, rather than in the hobby room, without upsetting your closest relatives. Very rarely are we facing big sawing or sanding jobs and models made from Styrofoam or Depron often do not even need painting any more.

In most cases Parkflyers are not very big either and a table with 100x30cm is big enough to prepare the components. Only the final assembly will require a bit more space in some cases. This limited space can also be found in a small house or a flat and we do not necessarily need a room that must have the dimensions of a ballroom for the assembly of the model.

A few different screwdrivers, a really sharp knife and some rulers are sufficient to produce a custom design. All these are things that can be found in every house. Apart from that, we

require some glues, depending on the material used. After a few years of building models, the number of different glues that are the modeller becomes familiar with is quite amazing, especially if different basic materials like wood and Depron are in use. The same applies for the different kinds of colours. Luckily enough this stock of glues and paints will build up slowly with every model build. Actually, in the beginning only a few things are required. It is nice to have a set of scales with a resolution of 1-2 grams to check the weight of the model and to check the results of actions taken to reduce the weight of a model. Such scales, even the digital ones, can be obtained quite cheaply as kitchen accessories. Wouldn't that be a nice Christmas gift with double purpose?

Other tools or equipment are not strictly required for Parkflyers, especially if you start with a kit for the first model. The fact, that so little equipment is needed for a Parkflyer is one of the reasons why they are so popular for beginners. It is only necessary to invest in the model, and the radio control without the need to spend a lot of money for tools or move the living room into the garage, just to have enough room for the first model.

Kit or building from scratch?

It is the personal decision of every modeller, whether to build a model from a kit or to start an own design from scratch. Some people just do not have the time and motivation to build a model from scratch and they are happy to buy a model with a high degree of pre-assembly in a model shop. Others just can't find the right model that suits their ideal, but want to see their ideas tested in reality. If even the huge number of different models available on the market does not fulfil their demands perfectly, there is no other way than to build a plane according to those ideas. Although most kits for Parkflyers won't cost more than £50-70, even this sum is too high for many modellers, considering the fact that an own design will definitely cost much less than that. This might be the final fact that leads to an own design.

Designing and building your own Parkflyer, is not all that difficult, once you are familiar with the techniques and the equipment that will need to be installed. If you have built models close to the upper weight limit for models though, it will be hard to be in the right frame of mind to save weight in a model that weighs only 2 percent of that. But it is quite easy to think in individual grams, once the scales are always at hand and frequently used.

It only takes a small amount of time and money to design a Parkflyer that will bring lots of fun in flying later on. Plans are widely available, as well in the model magazines and also on the internet. The models are simple designs, so that even a beginner can build his own Parkflyer from a plan without a problem. A Parkflyer also does not require absolute perfection and precision in building and a small inaccuracy will not show too much in flight. Most models are extremely forgiving. This encourages own designs even more, doesn't it?

Therefore the advice from the writer is simple: build your first Parkflyer from a kit and try to learn as much from that kit for a later own design. Then try your first own-design Parkflyer. Even if the first attempt fails, you do not lose too much, and you learn a lot to improve your next own design.

CHAPTER THREE

Model Categories

The big group of Parkflyers can be subdivided into further categories and you should look at the specialities of these individually to select the right model for yourself.

Each category has different flying characteristics and demands different requirement from the Pilot, the equipment and as well to the location where they can be flown. But this is one of the most interesting challenges in park flying. It has so many different aspects, that there are always new temptations and always new reasons to buy or build a further model.

Gliders

In the narrowest sense of park flying, a model without a motor can barely be though of as a Parkflyer, but nevertheless a glider is also capable of flying in confined spaces under certain circumstances and as long as it has a high degree of manoeuvrability.

It does not require a mini HLG (hand launch glider) with only 100 cm of wingspan to fly successfully on a football field or in a park. Even a normal HLG with 150cm or an "Unlimited HLG" can be thrown and flown in such areas by a skilled Pilot. Only the safety aspect of flying should be kept in mind if a glider is launched by hand or with the help of

a bungee to reach bigger altitudes.

Once launched, the varying surfaces of the site can offer interesting possibilities for thermal lift. For landing, a lawn is normally better that paved ground, as a glide normally doesn't carry landing gear and hard ground leaves ugly marks on the fuselage. Even if gliders are suitable for park flying, they will only play a small role in this book. They are a class of their own and the reader will easily find more detailed information about gliders in alternative sources.

Simple Parkflyers

This group covers the largest part of the Parkflyers available. As described earlier, the classic, simple Parkflyer is motorised and carries landing gear.

Simple Parkflyers are controlled by the rudder and the elevator, which is quite sufficient to achieve good manoeuvrability for flying in a limited space. Due to a low wing load between 10 and 20g/sq.dm the typical flying speed is low and only little space is needed to fly circles with this model.

On the other hand, these controls will not allow aerobatics apart from looping, a turn and other basic figures. Furthermore the power of the motor used in such a model will

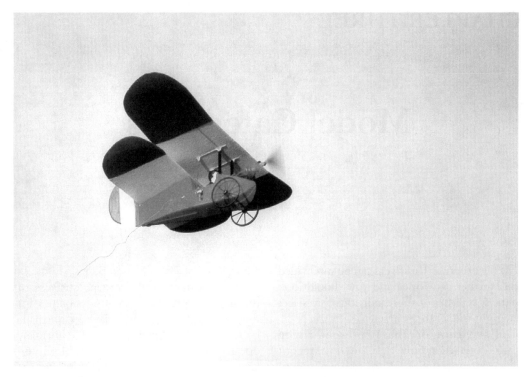

The Pou du Salle by IMA Belgium is a fine flyer with a unique design.

not allow more advanced aerobatics. They are designed rather for slow flying at low altitudes and precision flying where the street light, trees and other "obstacles" turn into challenges for the Pilot.

Due to their well balanced flying properties and the restrained way of flying, they are also suitable for beginners willing to learn flying motorised models. Once the student has practised clean takeoffs, landing and "touch-and-go" on a small parking area he will also be able to fly and land bigger models later on.

A further advantage lies in the relatively long flight time that can be achieved from one battery charge due to efficient drive trains.

Aerobatic Parkflyers

Sooner or later some Pilots may find it boring to fly slow circles over a car park and the wish for an aerobatic model will arise. With the right motor set-up even an expert model Pilot will be amazed looking at the figures an experienced Pilot can perform. Loops and turns are not that difficult, but rolls, cuban eights and inverted flying are possible and even if real power is required for a torque roll, this is possible with the right drive train. The most significant difference between a "normal" Parkflyer and an aerobatics model lies in the wing profile. For aerobatics more than a simple curved plate is required. Symmetrical profiles are the key to good performance in aerobatics and there are techniques to build such wings with low weights too. With such a wing, inverted flying and perfect rolls are much easier and look better than with simple mode'

Another difference is of course number of control surfaces. For aerc' ailerons are a MUST, while rudder c

The Robbe Lo 100 not only looks good, she also flys nicely.

also required. The need for ailerons is obvious, while the rudder in some models is a bonus. This doesn't apply to aerobatic models whether they be Parkflyers or others. A clean turn and knife-edge are only possible with a controlled rudder and even a simple take off can be difficult without.

More advanced aerobatic figures also require far more power from the motor. Plus, the battery that is supposed to supply the motor is also heavier. The model will be heavier than a plain Parkflyer and also faster. This requires more space for flying and landing. In narrow locations, this might demand too much from an inexperienced Pilot. Therefore the "learner" should only start to fly an aerobatic Parkflyer when he feels absolutely comfortable with a slow Parkflyer. Speed makes flying space appear smaller, this should be kept in mind at all times. On the positive side, a slightly heavier model can withstand a bit of wind much better.

Scale Parkflyers

Besides the purpose-built Parkflyers scale models have soon found their place in the scene. Especially for slightly bigger and heavier models, designers have soon looked around and successfully found prototypes that can easily be converted to Parkflyers. Especially the Simprop range of WW1 fighter planes has quickly found its place in the shops and on the flying fields. It was a wise decision to choose originals dating from that time. The engineers in those days also designed planes with large wing areas as the available profiles and engines were dependent on low wing loads to fly properly. In addition to that, Simprop launched a range of aerobatic Parkflyers that is also very interesting.

A simple Parkflyer with a hot design: the Liteflyer.

With 50 cm wingspan and controlled via all three axes, the Depron Pitts is a real aerobatic model for indoor flying.

The Extra 300S by Simprop is an aerobatic flyer as well as a scale oriented Parkflyer.

In the meantime there are a lot of Parkflyer kits available, that are more or less close to the original planes of the golden ages of flying. Looking for more modern originals for a Parkflyer we can turn to the very active ultralight scene, as here too, the originals have quite low power motors and must be very light to have an acceptable wing loading.

If the right plane cannot be found within these two categories, you will have to look for the right original in other places accepting, that a bit of cheating might be necessary to build a real Parkflyer and not a park racer. Of course building light is a must but in most cases this is insufficient and we won't get away without enlarging the wing area a bit. There are two ways to do this. Either the wingspan will be enlarged or alternatively the chord of the wing must grow. A bigger wing chord has the advantage that the model can fly slower, but there is a limit dictated by the appearance of the final model. The compromise is enlarge both the wingspan and the chord of the wing.

If they are increased carefully with the same factor, there is a good chance that the cheating remains unnoticed by most spectators. Only in very rare cases, will it be possible to design a Parkflyer absolutely to scale, but as long as a spectator recognises the original in the model, the effort was worthwhile.

Further compromises will be necessary when it comes to details like the wheels or the propellers, but once the wing load is in the right order, the rest can be adapted.

On the other hand a Parkflyer is a satisfying scale model, because the low flying speed of the Parkflyer is far more to scale than most "normal" scale models that are much too fast in the air compared to the original.

Regardless of the necessary compromises, it makes sense to design a Parkflyer to model an original plane and it will always pay to invest a little more time an effort in scale details.

So, whatever category of Parkflyers we are looking at, each has advantages and challenges and none are boring .

CHAPTER FOUR

The Propulsion Systems

Apart from the exceptional case of the pure gliders, our Parkflyers need a suitable motor and a propeller in order to lift off. The essential point in selecting the right propulsion set for a Parkflyer lies in the combination of motor, batteries, propeller and finally the model.

There must be a match between motor and propeller at the given voltage of the battery, in order to make sure, that the motors will work with the best possible efficiency. Are we demanding too little? In which case we waste weight, because we can get away with a lighter motor. Are we demanding too much? The motor will use a lot of the available energy to produce heat only and in worst case will die! Furthermore the drive train must be suitable for the model. A small and fast model of a Spitfire isn't at all suited to a big propeller rotating at low rpm's and a slow Parkflyer would be as wrong with a direct driven propeller at high rpm. Nevertheless both alternatives have their advantages and their reason for existence.

Direct drives

Direct drives are rarely found in a slow Parkflyer, as it is hard to find a light and small electric motor producing enough torque to swing a big propeller for a Parkflyer. On the other hand a direct drive is lighter than a motor with a gearbox and it is significantly quieter as we normally will only hear the sound of the propeller. Out of the huge number of available electric motors, we should take a closer look at the most popular ones.

Speed 280

The Graupner Speed 280 is THE Parkflyer-motor. Even if it is mostly used in conjunction with a gearbox. Nevertheless the Speed 280 can also be used as a direct drive motor. The most popular propeller in this case is the famous Günther design. With this propeller the Speed 280 draws about 3 Amps from an 8-cell Nickel Cadmium (Nicad) Battery and using the Sanyo 350mAH cells we have a nice propulsion for a quick Parkflyer weighing up to about 350 grams. In a fast model, where

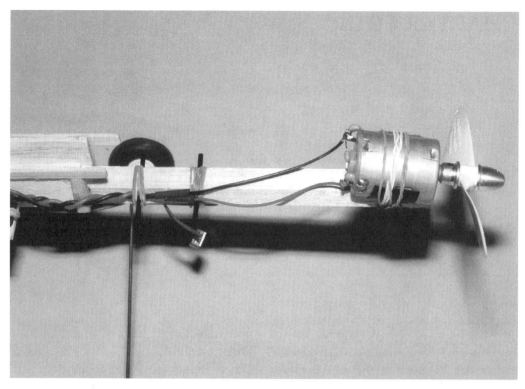

A Speed 280 in direct drive mode on the Lightflyer.

the current is reduced in flight, it is also possible to use 280 mAh Nickel Metal Hydride (NiMH) cells instead that will reduce weight by about 40 grams. Even the 110 mAh NiCd can be used, but then flying time goes down to about 3 minutes.

The direct drive Speed 280 is also very good for twin engine models. The prices are moderate and it is easy to fly a 600g model with two Speed 280 motors fitted with Günter propellers. A big advantage in this case is the fact that the sound of two direct Speed 280's is very nice and it is a pleasure to hear a model humming through the air like that.

Whenever we speak about a Speed 280 in this book, we should not forget, that the same motor is also available from Simprop and Robbe and the data mentioned apply for all versions.

Speed 400

Writing about the Speed 400 is nearly superfluous. A complete scene of electric flying has built up around this motor and it is amazing the variety of models that have been designed for this small and cheap powerplant. In direct drive the Speed 400 is nearly too fast for a Parkflyer and can only be used with battery packs using 6 or 7 cells in a Parkflyer. The right propeller is again the 125 mm Günther that is unbeaten in regards to the price/performance ratio and due to its flexibility, this propeller survives most model crashes too. Nearly an investment for life at a price of £1 only.

Speed 600 ECO

The Speed 600 ECO is not a real Parkflyer motor any more, just because it is both too heavy and too big for a Parkflyer. Due to the low current draw the Speed 600 ECO can be used as a direct drive motor together with small batteries and plays in the same league as a Speed 400 or 480 with a gearbox. The fascinating thing with this motor is the lack of noise and of course the fact that he has an extremely long life expectancy when used in the area of best efficiency around 10-12 Amps.

Geared power drives

The majority of Parkflyers are driven by a geared motor, as the advantages of a gearbox are evident. Due to the reduction, the motor can swing a much bigger propeller with a much greater efficiency and only this higher efficiency made it possible to fly the first Slowflyers at all, although there was the disadvantage of the weight of the gearbox.

In addition to the higher efficiency of the big propeller, a big propeller turning at low revolutions is better suited to the character of the slow Parkflyer than a small propeller at high turns. The big propeller produces a slow airflow that is closer to the flying speed of the model.

Again we will take a closer look at the most popular motors in the field.

Speed 400 with Günther propeller – a popular direct drive combination.

Speed 280

As mentioned before, most Speed 280's in Parkflyers are combined with a gearbox and the geared 280 is the standard Parkflyer drive

The Multiplex Pico Cub is driven with a Rondo 400; a Speed 400 with a circular Kontronik Controller attached to the backplate.

The Slofly 240 drive set is very effective, but this quality has a price.

for most models. With a weight of 42grams without and 65-75grams with a gearbox and a propeller, the Speed 280 is a good motor for Parkflyers up to about 400grams. The motor feels comfortable, when it draws about 2-3 Amps. The maximum should be around 5 Amps for a Speed 280. Suitable reduction ratios are between 3:1 to 4,5:1 Greater reductions would demand too big a propeller with low rpm and a very slow airflow.

6-8 Cells 110-600 mAH are the right power supply for this little power plant. 10 cells are also possible, but then the motor is at the limit and close to burnout.

The slightly stronger version is the Speed 280 RACE from Graupner that is in the same price band but it can turn out a bit more power than the regular 280 closing the gap to the Speed 300.

Permax 280BB / Speed 280BB

The Permax 280BB from Multiplex is the upmarket version of the 280. Same dimensions, but 3-4 times higher in price characterise this motor with ball bearings and exchangeable brushes. The Speed 280BB is running at such high revolutions, that it makes no sense to use it without a gearbox, but with a reduction of 5:1 and 8 cells this motor can move. Although the motor has the highest efficiency at about 3,5 Amps, it can easily handle 5 Amps and even with 7 Amps for a short time. A larger NiMH battery of 6-8 cells with a capacity of 350 to 600 mAh, is also possible and with 8 Sanyo N500 AR cells, a 5:1 reduction and a 10x4,7in APC Slowprop the match is just right. Even a Graupner Sunwheel biplane at 550grams is well motorised with this combination.

Speed 300

The Speed 300 motor is the money saving alternative to the Speed 280BB if a motor in the size bracket of the Speed 280 is foreseen but more power is required. This motor can handle even more Amps than the Speed

The Simprop Speed 300 drive set. The capacitors are absolutely necessary to reduce the interference from the motor that could affect the receiver.

280BB but the low price has an effect on the maximum efficiency. This is the only explanation for the fact, that the Sunwheel has about 3 minutes more flying time with the Speed 280BB compared to the Speed 300.

The Speed 300 easily consumes 8-10 Amps with a propeller, that is just a little bit too big and for this a different Electronic Speed Controller (ESC) is required. Nevertheless we should refrain from this and make sure, that no more than about 6 Amps will flow through the connections. This will be very positive for the life expectancy of the motor, otherwise the brushes will be gone after 30-50 flights. Apart from that, the 350 mAh cells are at a maximum with 6 Amps and for higher currents the Sanyo N500 AR cells must be used as only they can provide this power safely.

The gearbox should offer a reduction not under 4,5:1, otherwise the possible propellers are getting too small. On the positive side even with 6 cells impressive aerobatics are possible. The Speed 300 is more suitable for fast aerobatic models than for slow biplanes. In the Graupner Sunwheel, the Speed 280BB was the better choice. In the Simprop Extra the Speed 300 has proven to be nearly ideal, if full power is only applied for short moments when required.

Speed 400

Again! A lot has been said about this motor, and we do not need to add much more. In direct driven fast models it is superb, but it can also be used with a gearbox for big Parkflyers and other slow models. With 6 cells a small reduction of 1,8:1 is suitable, with seven and eight cells the gearbox ratio may go up to 4,5:1. The right batteries would range from 500mAh up to 1600mAh NiMH cells.

With such combinations, models up to a weight of about 1000grams can fly safely.

Sure enough some readers would like to know more details about this matter, but unfortunately we do not have enough room to show everything. But the model industry does not leave us standing in the rain at this point, and a lot of well tested complete drive sets are available on the market consisting of motor, gearbox and the right propeller together with a suggestion for the battery. In the majority of cases these sets are good and reliable so that they can be used without hesitation, and even if you do not want to buy a complete set, the information about the components of the sets are very useful and can be taken as a guideline.

The following drive sets have actually been used by the author.

Complete propulsion sets

Ikarus Parkflyer set

The Ikarus Parkflyer drive set consists of a Speed 280 Motor with a 3,3:1 gearbox and 2 special propellers of about 10in diameter. It should be used with 6-8 cells providing sufficient power from 6 cells due to the relatively low gear ratio and the big propeller for slow models with about 300g. With eight cells 350 mAh even 400gram models will fly properly.

At first sight, the gearbox seems to be rather primitive but against all doubts it works nicely at an unbeatable price. The propellers are not just High-Tech, but after thorough balancing they do a very good job and do not produce too much noise.

Simprop Park Drive 300

This set contains a Speed 280 with a 4:1 gearbox and a 10x4,7in APC Slowprop. With 8 cells the WW1 Depron Parkflyers from Simprop or Robbe are well motorised if the weight stays around 300grams. For heavier models a 10x7in Slowprop can be used instead.

This drive set was the basis of a complete range of gearboxes with reduction ratios of 4:1; 4,5:1; 5:1 and 6:1 that accept motors with an outside diameter from 22,8-24,4mm. Namely these are the Speed 280, Speed 300 and Speed 280BB. Completely equipped, i.e. with motor and propeller the drive sets have a weight of 65-80grams and they are suitable for models between 250 and 600grams. A wide range that can be flown with these lightweight drive sets.

The gearboxes are designed to accept the APC Slowprops, that are available from Robbe as well as from Simprop and Kavan. Furthermore, Jamara is offering these gearboxes without a motor. The possible combination can be summarised in the following scheme.

Simprop Acro Drive 350

This drive set was especially designed for the Simprop Acro Parkflyers like the SU31 or the Extra 330S. It comes with a 9x6in propeller to provide enough speed for these models. In a slower Parkflyer should it be flown with a 10x4,7in propeller.

Robbe drive sets

As mentioned before, motors similar to the Speed 280 and Speed 300 as well as the gearboxes described before are also available from Robbe. The data and recommendations given before apply to these drive sets as well, but there is a little difference!

Simprop supplies an M8 polyamide locknut with the gearbox while Robbe has a metal locknut. The plastic nut can easily be tightened by hand, while the metal nut requires a wrench, a pair of pliers or any other tool to secure the propeller. We should refrain from that, because the nut could be over-tightened this way. With too much torque the bell of the gearbox is distorted and can tighten up. This again causes heat and the melting of the material will cause permanent damage to the gearbox. In any case the axle of the gearbox should be lubricated before the first test run. The author drills a small hole in the bell to lubricate the gearbox without dismantling.

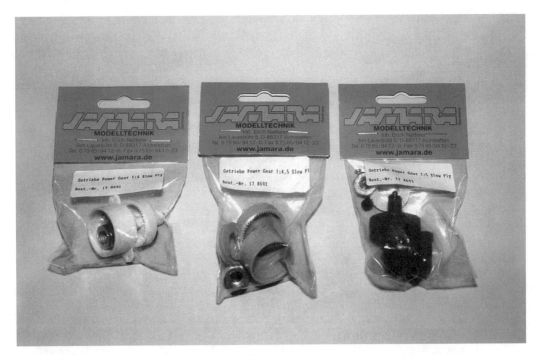

Three Parkflyer gearboxes by Jamara with different reductions. Similar gearboxes are also available from Robbe and Simprop.

This reduces the noise and increases the durability of the gearbox.

Graupner Speed 280FG3

This drive set forms the power train for the Parkflyers from Graupner. The chosen reduction ratio of 3:1 is rather low and for this reason only propellers with a diameter of 8 or 9 inches can be used which means, that the drive set is rather low on power for models like Pepito, Sunwheel or Fokker EIII. But for smaller and lighter models around 300grams the power is sufficient.

The lower gear ratio and the resulting higher rpm of the propeller also causes a higher noise level than most other gearboxes.

Pusteblume by MTM

Mike's Tiny Models in Göttingen, Germany has specialised in propulsion sets for lighter electric models i.e. Slowflyers and Parkflyers focusing on a very high quality. Unfortunately this quality also has an effect on the price, but that is inevitable.

Pilots who are seriously interested in Slow and Parkflyers should definitely look into the MTM catalogue, as this does not only provide product information. A big chapter giving a lot of useful information for the motorization of light electric models can also be found here. The Pusteblume is about the smallest drive set in this line and it is designed for the light ones among the Parkflyers up to a weight of about 200-220grams. The biggest advantages are the light weight of about and of course the smooth run. Due to the high reduction the small motor can swing propellers up to 9x4,7in or even 10x4,7in

S240 Slowfly by MTM

According to the manufacturer this drive set produces about 180g of thrust with a 10x4,7in propeller if power comes from an 8 cell pack

This is about as much thrust, as we can get from a Speed 280 with gearbox and

Graupner Speed 280 FG3 with a 3:1 reduction.

therefore sufficient for models up 350g of weight. Due to the thick main gear and the ball bearing the drive set runs absolutely silently and gives the impression that it is made for eternity. Unfortunately this durability is not for free.

WASP drive set by MTM

The WASP is a drive set with a Speed 280BB motor, a 5:1 reduction and a very interesting three-blade-propeller with the dimension 9x9in. This means that we are looking at a quite fast airflow, just right for an aerobatic model up to 400g. Even more thrust can be obtained from a huge 11x7in Slowprop.

Eight cells with 350 mAh or 500 mAh have to supply a current of 5-6 Amps which means that the 350 mAh cells are at their limit. For more power, that the motor handles easily, high current 500 mAh cells are absolutely required. Then models even over 500grams are well motorised. With 1600mA Twicell

flight times up to 20 minutes are also possible, if this is the target.

Simprop Basic Drive 400+

According to the Simprop catalogue this set consisting of a Speed 400, a 3,66:1 gearbox and a 10x7in Slowprop is sufficient for models up to 600g. The author can confirm this statement, even slightly heavier models can be flown with this combination. In any case a 550g Sunny Boy is well motorised with this set and the best thing about it is the non-existent sound of the gearbox. This won't upset any neighbour at all.

Due to the high reduction, the relatively big propeller is turning at low RPM and therefore very effectively. A speciality is the flexible mounting of the propeller, allowing it to move aside, when the ground is touched. This takes away a lot of stress from the gearbox, the propeller and also the model in general.

The Groß Wasp can barely be seen behind the huge three bladed propeller.

Simprop Fun Drive 450+

Fitting a stronger motor to the above mentioned Basic Drive means more power for heavier models up to 800grams, while maintaining the good properties of the gearbox. The 800grams quoted by Simprop has been confirmed in practical application and even the higher revolutions of the propeller do not increase the noise level in operation.

How much power?

How much power is required in relation to the all-up weight? Looking into several articles written in past magazines, the authors opinion has been confirmed, that a typical Parkflyer will need about 8 Watts of input power for every 100grams of flying weight.

In the old days of electric flying there was a rule of thumb saying, that about 100 Watt/kilo, i.e. 10 Watt/100gram is required for flying. We are not so far away from that. The difference can be explained by the fact, that most Parkflyers are using a gearbox to reduce the revolutions of the propeller in order to increase the efficiency.

Based on this assumption the following list can be produced indicating which motor and which battery is suitable to convert an aircraft model of a given weight into a flying model.

Using the list the weight of the complete drive train, i.e. motor, gearbox, propeller and battery has be considered in order to make clear, that a wrong set-up might end meaning that there is no more weight left for the model as such.

In order to see how much weight can be allowed for the model and the controls, the weight of the drive train therefore has to be subtracted from the total weight. After that, we come to the list as printed below.

47

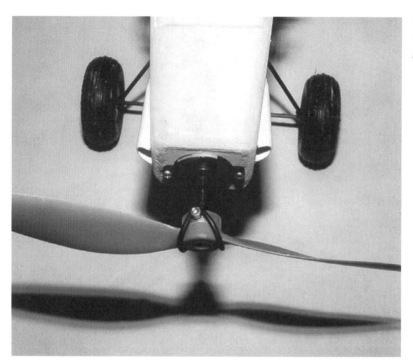

The Simprop Basic 400 has a flexible propeller mount.

With the help of the list it is quite easy to identify the possibilities given with the planned or existing drive set and if the plane gets heavier after all, the new drive set for the given weight can also be found.

Anyway, it has to be stressed, that 8 Watt/100g is sufficient for "normal" flying. This means a safe lift off from the ground, a secure climb and enough power for a loop or a turn. Real aerobatics require about

If power is not sufficient the Simprop Fun Drive 450 provides additional thrust.

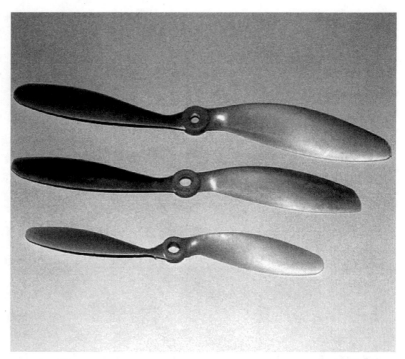

A selection of APC Slowprops specially developed for the rpm and output power of Parkflyer style electric power.

double the power, if you really want fun.

The right propeller

Besides the motor and the gearbox, the propeller is an essential part of the drive train.

For quite a time there have been dedicated propellers for slow and Parkflyers that have a specially low weight. Normal propellers are designed for much stronger motors and they have to withstand a lot of vibration if they

A GWS Slowprop driven by the Grost Pusteblume.

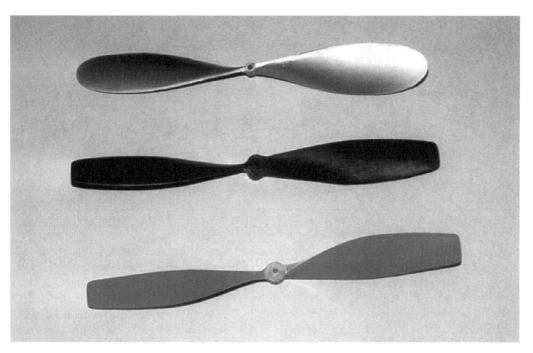

Simple propellers originating from free flight rubber driven models are also suitable for Parkflyers.

On the left-hand side we have the famous Günther Propeller with a Graupner precision Spinner and on the right there is the Graupner three blade propeller for the Speed 280.

are used with an IC motor.

In a Parkflyer, the propeller is turning at much lower rpm, at least when a reduction is used and there are basically no vibrations at all. Therefore they can be made much thinner and also lighter. This was first recognised by APC and they launched a big range of Slowprops with low pitch which are also very good for slow models. In the meantime GWS from Taiwan are also producing similar propellers with a characteristic orange colour.

With a bit of effort, it is also possible to find propellers that were originally designed for rubber-powered free-flight models, that are also suitable for Parkflyers.

Apart from that, very exclusive hand-made carbon propellers can be found on the market that are very strong and very light, but also very expensive. Probably you can find the last bit of efficiency with these propellers, but it is questionable, whether they are worth the price.

For direct drive some small propellers,

designed for IC motors can be found in the marketplace that are suitable for the Speed 280, but here we have to have a close look at the current when testing not to let it rise too high.

Absolutely famous, the white 125mm Günther propeller is also widely used by the Speed 400 scene, just because it is so cheap and good. Unfortunately it doesn't fit as well on the 2,0 mm shaft of the Speed 280 as on the 2,3 mm shaft of the Speed 400. For this reason it should be considered for use with an aluminium holder from Graupner instead of the rubber spinner originally supplied with the propeller.

Careful clipping of the Günther propeller reduces the current and takes a bit of load from the small 280 motor prolonging its life significantly.

The Graupner 5x2in grey propeller as well as the small 3-blade propeller from Graupner are also suitable for the Speed 280 producing a bit less thrust than the Günther propeller.

For the Tipsy, Graupner designed a folding propeller just right for the Speed 280.

Chapter Five

Batteries for Parkflyers

The power supply for the motor plays an important role in a Parkflyer as the weight of the battery is the most significant element in the model. In most Parkflyer the batteries is even heavier than the motor or the radio components. Therefore it is essential to select the right battery for a Parkflyer.

The power supplies for Parkflyers can roughly be divided into three groups. Firstly Nickel Cadmium cells (NiCd), these are still most commonly used. Following these are the Nickel Metal Hydride Cells (NiMh) that have taken over a lot of applications recently and finally we have the Lithium Ion and Lithium Polymer Cells (Li-Po) that can be used, with limitations, for Parkflyers too.

Nickel Cadmium Cells (NiCd)

This type of battery has been in the marketplace for many years and is still the most important battery for electric flying. They are famous for their robustness in discharging as well as in charging. There are many chargers available on the market for this type of battery and the technology is widely understood, so that most chargers available will charge NiCd's. Another reason for their popularity is the fact, that they have a low internal resistance and therefore NiCd's won't

come to any harm, even if they are discharged a high rates.

Stop! Many readers will now think, that our Parkflyer motors don't take such high currents compared to other electric flying Models. Unfortunately there is a big error in this assumption. While the current as such, between 2 - 8 Amps is actually not that high if we are looking and 30, 50 or even 80 Amps in other models, the discharge ratio in relation to the capacity of the battery is actually very high. The experts talk about the C-Rate looking at the relation between the current drawn and the capacity of the battery.

Let us look at a small example. If we discharge a Sub-C cell with 2400 mAh capacity at a rate of 2,4 Amp, we have a C-Rate of 1C. The battery could provide this current for one hour. In this case 24 Amps are 10C and 48 Amps are 20C. Converting this calculation to a 350 mAh cell we see, that quite normal 3,5 Amps are 10 C and flying aerobatics in a Parkflyer at 7 Amps means 20 C.

With this in the background it is questionable to supply a Speed 280 at a current of 3 Amps from 110 mAh cells, just in order to have a light model. The battery is definitely not happy in this situation and even if we take good care of the battery, we cannot expect too many discharge cycles like that from the battery.

For this reason we should keep the C-Rate in mind when selecting the battery for a Parkflyer. This way a longer service life of the battery can be expected and longer flight times per battery are also possible.

Most NiCd batteries are so robust, that they can live with a 10C discharge even in the long term and a top load of 15C doesn't do any harm, if the model is not flown at full speed all the time.

When charging NiCd's the current can go up to 4C. This means, that the battery is fully charged in about 20 minutes, but the batteries are likely to last longer if the charge rate does not exceed 2C.

It is also good for the batteries, if they are allowed to cool down to room temperature before charging as well as before flying. Even better, if they do not get hot at all.

So much about the positive sides of the NiCd cells. Unfortunately there are also some negative aspects, mainly the fact, that they suffer badly from the so-called "Memory Effect", if they are not discharged completely before re-charging. Loss of capacitiy is a clear sign of the "Memory Effect".

Good battery care is the most important thing for NiCd's. This means, that they should be completely discharged before charging and that they should be conditioned from time to time by charging the pack at only 0,1C for at least 24 hours.

The following is a brief overview of the most popular types of NiCd cells. Cells with 110 and 120mAh capacity are, in common with the 50mAh cells, are only suitable for very light Parkflyers or indoor models. The maximum current for the 50mAh cells is about 1 Amp and for the 110 or 120mAh cells it is 3 Amps for a short time.

Just right for Parkflyers especially for the geared Speed 280 motors are the 250, 280 and 350 mAh cells, especially the Sanyo N350 AAC

that has taken over this sector more or less completely. Even a Speed 280BB, consuming not more than 6-7 Amps at full speed can be used with these cells.

Batteries like the Sanyo N500 AR or the N600 AE are just right for Speed 400 models or for Speed 280BB and Speed 300 at higher loads. The Sanyo N600 AE is the high capacity cell in the group with a maximum current of 8 Amps while the N500 AR is a robust cell for providing high currents up to 12-14 Amps without a problem. Bigger NiCd cells are not adviseable for Parkflyers as they are too heavier and most Parkflyer do not have enough structural strengh to cope with the higher weight. If more capacitiy is required, other technologies are demanded.

Nickel-Metal-Hydride Cells (NiMH)

The Nickel Metal Hydride cells have been developed in the course of the last few years in order to store more electrical energy in the same volume and for the same weight. Years ago, a typical AA cell had a capacity of 600mAh while modern NiMH cells are available at same dimensions and about the same weight with 2200mAh now which is proven by the Sanyo HR3 U cells impressively. Another example: A typical NiCd AAA cell has a capacity of 250mAh while the NiMH Cell at the same dimension has 700mAh . This a such is significant progress but in addition to that, NiMH cells are suffer much less from memory effect.

Taking these two points into consideration the question comes up, why NiCd's are still in use at all. The internal resistance of the NiMh cell is the crucial point so far, as it is higher than with NiCd cells. Therefore NiCd cells are still more suited for high discharge rates. 5C is still O.K. for NiMh cells, but 10C is too much in most cases. This is no reason for panic taking into consideration that 5C for the 700mAh NiMH

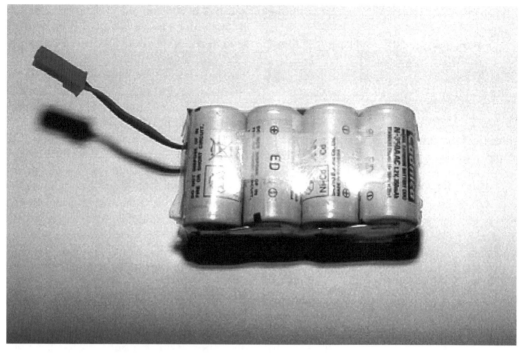

Eight cells of Sanyo 350 AAC. A small powerpack for Parkflyers.

Twicell equates to 3,5A . That same 3,5 Amps would mean 16C though for the Sanyo N250 AAA at the same dimension. Changing from NiCd to NiMh in this case means the same dimension and weight for the battery but a longer flying time.

The second disadvantage comes from the voltage level of the NiMh cells under load which is lower than with NiCd's at the same current. As a rule of thumb, it can be said that 8 NiMh cells at 3,5 Amps load would have the same voltage as a 7 cell NiCd pack. Therefore most modellers would have one NiMh cell more on board than with a NiCd Pack.

For the same reason, we should refrain from using the higher capacity of the NiMh cells to produce more power by more Amps. NiMH cells are the long distance runners, while NiCd's are the sprinters.

Due to the higher internal resistance, the cells also tend to get warmer in discharge and in charging than NiCd cells. Again there is no reason for concern, but the NiMh cells should be given enough time to cool down before they get charged again.

Regarding charging techniques; the NiMh's are also a bit more sensitive than their older relations, as the drop in voltage at the end of the charge that is used by the Delta Peak charger to sense the fully charged state is not that significant and sometimes even not visible at all. Most recent chargers have special charging programs for NiMH cells but it is generally advisable to have an eye on this feature when buying a charger. The charge rate should not exceed 2C, so about 35-40 minutes are required to charge a NiMh battery, but waiting is worthwhile anyway, as we are also looking at longer flying times.

The development of NiMh cells is not yet so far advanced as with the NiCd and we

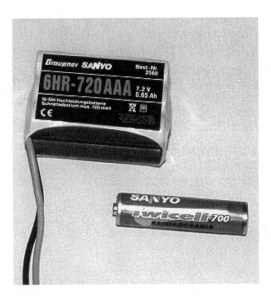

The Sanyo Twicell 750 as an individual cell as well as a six cell pack.

are surely still on the way to better cells . In the meantime the GP company has succeeded producing a 600mAh cell with a weight slightly higher than the Sanyo Twicell that is able to supply 9 Amps at an acceptable voltage and at full capacity. This can be taken as a proof, that we will soon see even better NiMH cells on the market.

Lithium Polymer Cells (LiPo)

Despite the above, future has already begun for slow and Parkflyers.

With the advent of Lithium Polymer (LiPo) batteries, the future of Parkflying is here already. Due to their higher voltage of 3,6-3,7 Volts per cell, only two or three cells are required to power a Parkflyer and we benefit from a significant saving in weight for the model.

Unfortunately LiPo cells are slightly more expensive than NiCad or NiMh cells and they are also more prone to damage if they are used outside their specification. There are three things they do not like at all. First of all they should not be discharged completely. A

voltage of 3,0 Volts per cell is the minimum level for discharge if the life of the batteries is to be longer than 30 or 50 cycles.

Secondly they must not be discharged at too high a current. On the market at the moment we find very different cells allowing discharge rates from 5C up to 20C. Serious suppliers of LiPo Cells for model flying would always quote two discharge rates in their specification.

One is the discharge rate for continuous discharge, the other one is for short term discharge. The period for "short term" though should be considered in the range of 2-5 seconds, otherwise we should only look at the long term discharge rate.

In practical application this means that an aerobatic model, normally flying at half throttle and only using full power for certain manouevres may use the full quoted 20C power of the batteries but we must not use the "short term" current for a regular model that needs 80% throttle or full power most of the time.

In order to get as much as possible out the cells, we should make sure, that the currents stay in the long term limit or lower, if possible.

The last matter to look at is charging of the LiPo batteries. Lithium Ion and Lithium Polymer cells can only be charged with special chargers. Although the technique required for charging LiPo cells is quite simple, the batteries are not forgiving at all in this matter and it is essential that a charger with a program for LiPo cells is used.

An error in charging might not only destroy the battery, but charged in the wrong way, LiPo cells may catch fire and there are cases reported, where these batteries have been the cause of destruction of cars and hobby rooms.

Therefore please double check your charger is set correctly and put the battery in a fire resistant environment with nothing else

Lithium Polymer Batteries - Weights and Capacities					
Name	Capacity mAh	Dimensions	Weight/cell	Discharge 1	Discharge 2
Kokam 360	350	2,7 x 34 x 52	11 g	10 A	6 A
Kokam 1500	1500	6,4 x 38 x 70	35 g	15 A	10 A
Kokam 2000	2000	9 x 43 x 74	52 g	30 A	20 A

that can burn in close proximity.

So much about the risks and disadvantages! Be assured, the future of electric model flying lies in LiPo cells despite the points mentioned above and Parkflyers are only the beginning. The reduction in weight is significant and the new technology makes models work that were critical before. In a few years from now they will have taken over completely and this development is only starting at the moment coming from small models like Parkflyers.

Apart from the weight reduction there is a final advantage of the new cells that should not be forgotten. The self discharge of the batteries is very low and we can charge the battery just after flying and use them two weeks later with the same power as freshly charged. Also the LiPo batteries do not experience a "memory effect" so they can be charged and discharged only half way without a problem.

Plugs and cables

Before we leave the area of propulsion, there is one more detail left that should not be forgotten. The plugs and cables. Generally, we are looking a currents of 2-3 Amps in connection with a Speed 280 but a Speed 280BB, a Speed 300 or a Speed 400 can draw 10-12 Amps easily.

Looking at the higher currents, the popular red 2-Pole BEC connectors with a cable diameter of 0,14 mm are unsuitable and we need to look at connectors that can withstand the higher currents without too much loss. A good compromise between technical features, weight and cost are the 2 mm gold connectors. The cable diameter should at least be 0,5 to 0,75 sq mm in order to keep the losses in an acceptable range. There is a perceptible gain in power with these connectors and cables and they are much safer securing better contact. If you ever had a plane crashing due to a BEC connector melting at 7 Amps, you will know what I mean.

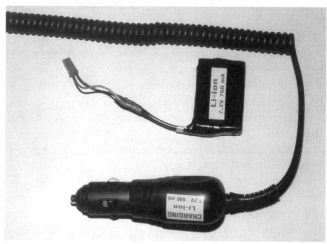

The Lithium Ion set from FVK with the battery and a suitable charger.

CHAPTER SIX

Chargers for Parkflyers

Finding a suitable charger for our Parkflyer batteries seems to be easy at first sight. If there is no problem in charging the 27 cell pack of a hotliner within 30 minutes at 8 Amps charging current, then it must be easy to charge 6or 8 small cells with a capacity of only 350mAh.

At a second glance, things are not that easy any more, just because most chargers we can find at the local hobby shop are capable of producing high charging currents rather than the low currents that are required for our batteries and in many cases, the lowest possible current is already quite high for us. At this point we come again to our charging and discharging rate C from above. Following please find a small chart showing which charging currents refer to the usual C rates in regards to Parkflyer batteries.

It must be pointed out, that a charge rate of 4C is the maximum for most Nickel-Cadmium cells and normally they should not be charged higher than 2C. Most manufacturers of batteries would even consider the above rates as high and higher charging currents are definitely Murder!

Nickel Metal Hydride cells are even more sensitive and 2C is the absolute maximum if they are to be useable for more than one summer.

The lower end of the charge rate should not be left aside either, because batteries cannot always be charged at high currents. From time to time a slow charge with 1/10C is required to balance a battery pack and secure a longer lifespan.

Therefore we must not be blinkered by the highest possible charging currents when looking for a suitable charger, but the low end must be kept in sight at all times. Looking at the catalogues and leaflets from this point of view, it becomes obvious that many chargers have a minimum current of 1 Amp, which is definitely too high. 500mAh should be the absolute maximum, even better if the charge current can be adjusted in steps of 100mA.

For battery care and formation a simple charger powered from the mains that can offer 25mA current as a minimum is sufficient. Even here the selection is not all that easy unless you want to spend a lot of money.

Following are descriptions of some chargers divided into two categories; 12V quick chargers amd mains electricity powered chargers.

Typical, simple 12 Volt input automatic charger from Kavan.

Quick chargers

Kavan Mini Charger

This small and handy unit has been designed especially for the needs of slow and Parkflyer pilots. With a dimension of 70x32x10mm it is extremely small and fits into every toolbox easily. The charging current can be adjusted with a "jumper" and covers batteries of 50-800mAh capacity at charge rates from 50mA to 1.5Amps. An LED indicates that the charger is working and when the LED blinks, the battery is fully charged and the charger has switched into a trickle charge mode.

Another positive point is the fact, that the charger is suitable for NiCd cells as well as for NiMh cells. The only point, that is a bit annoying is the fact, that the charger needs to be cut off from the power supply before every charge, which means, that we have to fiddle with the supply cable a lot. The solution would be a switch in the cable, but this is not an option described in the manual.

In practical application the Kavan Mini charger did handle all batteries connected and charged them with about 30 minutes being a good companion in the car on many flying opportuities. Unfortunately only 7 cells can be charged from 12Volts while at home with a 13,8Volt power supply even 8 cells can be charged.

Robbe Power Peak Slow Fly

Robbe has designed this charger especially for Parkflyer batteries keeping the cost aspect in mind. The charger is placed in an enclosure that doubles as the plug for the car cigar lighter socket. This mean the charger can easily be connected to the car battery. The connection to the Parkflyer batteries are made with the help of a long cable and 2 mm gold connectors.

The charging current is set to 650mA which is just right for batteries with 250-600

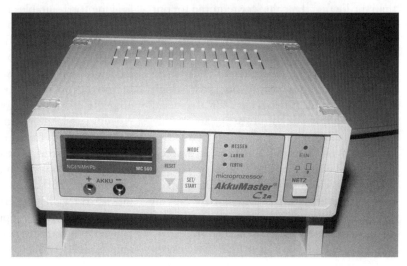

Conrad electronic supplies many chargers for home applications for 240 Volt mains supply.

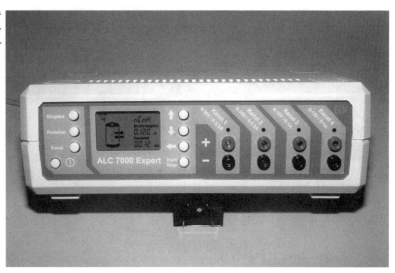

The ALC 7000 Expert from ELV is a very comfortable unit for home charging.

mAh with 6 or 7 cells. This is more or less exactly what is required for most Parkflyers.

The Power Peak Slow Fly has an intelligent control for the Indicator LED. While charging it is constantly on and a flashing shows that the battery is fully charged. In addition to that the flashing LED shows how much capacity has been pumped into the pack. Every flash stands for 50mAh, so 7 flashes indicate that 350mAh has been input. By this means we get an indication about the battery state and can be sure that the charger did not interrupt charging too early.

The special shape of the enclosure has both good and bad aspects. On one hand it is possible to charge the battery in the car, even on the way to the flying location as we don't need to open the car bonnet. On the other hand the lighter socket in most cars is only live whilst the ignition switch is on. This causes unnecessary consumption of energy and the danger of discharging the car battery completely, which is bad news for the journey home. Furthermore it is not all that easy to use the unit at home. Nevertheless a good idea introduced by Robbe, to produce a special charger for Parkflyers only and the price is

absolutely acceptable, so that the Power Peak Slow Fly can even be bought as a additional charger.

Mains Chargers with Cycling facility

Now we are turning to the "Rolls Royce" amongst chargers, the units that have sophisticated computers inside controlling the charging, discharging, cycling and other programs that are made to prolong the service lives of our batteries and keep them in top condition.

Conrad Electronics Akkumaster C3

The big electronic mail order shop Conrad has evolved into a big dealer for model accessories in recent years and offers a full range of chargers designed to suit our needs. As an example we are now looking at the Akkumaster C3 charger, that is sufficient for most applications. The charging current can be adjusted from 10mA up to 500mA and the same applies for the discharging currents. This means we can charge all batteries from 110 mAh to 350mAh even as a quick charge and bigger capacities can be conditioned with this unit as well. Altogether there are 9 different

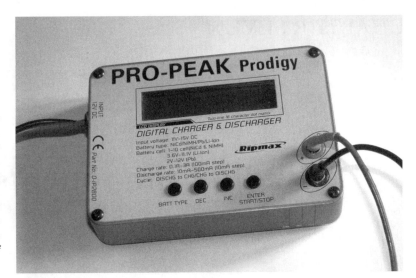

The Pro-Peak Prodigy is a middle priced 12 Volt input charger that can charge and discharge NiCd, NiMh and LiPo cells with an LCD screen displayto keep the user abreast of happenings.

programs such as Discharge-charge, Charge-discharge-charge and also real cycling programs , that will keep the Akkumaster busy for several days.

ELV ALC 7000 Expert

This upmarket version of a home charger is the ALC 7000 Expert from ELV, effectively 4 chargers in one box.

Of these 4 chargers, three can be used at the same time, because the channels No.1 and 2 are working alternatively with a maximum current of 3,5 A . Four batteries can be connected to the ALC 7000 at the same time, for example in the morning before you go to work and they will all be fully charged after work for a relaxed flying time in the garden. That sounds great, doesn't it?

In addition to that the ALC 7000 is again not only a charger, but a complete care station for batteries; that is charging, discharging and cycling. Basically all you need to keep your batteries fit. Importantly for Parkflyers, low currents can be handled, but the first two channels can charge with up to 3,5 A which is enough to charge Sub-C Cells within 30 minutes. The investment in this unit soon pays off, as it keeps the batteries under best possible condition.

CHAPTER SEVEN

Radio Components

As weight is an essential point for the flying properties of Parkflyers, they should also be equipped with lightweight radio equipment. Talking about this point, there are often misunderstandings with other model Pilots arguing against Parkflyers with the argument that Parkflyers need a lot of highly specialised and therefore expensive radio equipment . A few years ago, this argument was absolutely correct, but since then the industry has developed a lot of equipment in light versions at prices which are mostly under the prices of "normal " radio equipment.

Lightweight receivers under 20 grams are good quality and are in most cases, the cheapest around and the 5Amp speed controllers are also much lower in price than the controllers for 20 or 40 Amps. Finally the 6 gram servos today have come down to a similar price to normal servos in the medium price range. At around £75 a complete airborne pack consisting of a receiver, two servos and a speed controller can be obtained in a normal hobby shop round the corner. That is about the same price as a digital servo for a helicopter. Now let us take a look at the components individually.

Receivers

Basically all available receivers are suitable for Parkflyers, as long as they are not too heavy. We should set a limit around 20 grams including the crystal and the antenna. As Parkflyers rarely need more than three servos and the ESC, even simple receivers are sufficient.

In addition to the receivers that are designed to work within the full range of the transmitter, say about 1000 metres, most manufacturers also supply receivers that only guarantee a limited range. About 300 metres is definitely sufficient for a Parkflyer, visibility of these small models is the limiting factor.

Receivers with limited range
Simprop Indoor 2000
The Indoor 2000 by Simprop was one of the first receivers especially designed for a limited range on the marketplace. It weighs only 9 grams including the crystal and was unbeaten for a long time taking into consideration, that it had a full size crystal and normal Graupner/ JR servo connectors.

The reduced range of about 200 metres is still enough for a Parkflyer and so far the

author has not encountered serious problems that could be blamed on this receiver.

Simprop Micro Scan 4+1

This unit is a very special receiver on the market. Together with its smaller brother, the Micro Scan 4 the Micro Scan 4+1 do not need a crystal any more. With an inbuilt scanner these receivers lock on on the strongest signal they can find whilst in programming mode. Furthermore there is a 10Amp motor controller integrated into the unit, so that the motor can be plugged directly to the receiver. With a weight of 17 grams the Scan 4+1 is about as heavy as other receivers with a crystal and a 10 Amp ESC separately, but there are far fewer cables in the model.

Once the Micro Scan 4+1 is logged onto one frequency and has found the right channel

No more crystals required. The Simprop Micro Scan 4+1 receiver. The XP 8 FM by Graupner is a small and low-priced receiver for 4 Servos.

for the motor controller, which is not all that simple sometimes, it handles like any other receiver and there is nothing special to report. But sometimes no news is good news!

Multiplex Pico ¾

With the Micro ¾ Multiplex has shown how light a complete receiver with a case can be. The crucial point about this receiver is the choice of connectors. The special micro-connectors are very lightweight, but they also provide very good contact. Unfortunately it is a bit difficult to find servos with these connectors already fitted. This is one of the reasons, why many wholesalers do not offer this receiver at all. The same applies to the

The Becker SE88 combined receiver/ servo module with linear outputs.

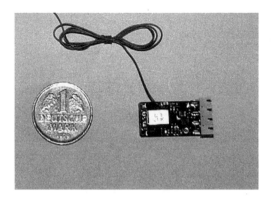

Presently the smallest and lightest receiver available The JMP RX 5-2,3 by WES Technik.

mini-crystals that reduce the weight of the Pico ¾ significantly. In practical applications no problems with this receiver have occurred.

Graupner XP8 FM

This receiver is presently about the smallest affordable receiver on the market. The scale only shows 6,9 grams including antenna and crystal, which is slightly above the catalogue weight, but the difference doesn't really count. Another positive is the fact that it uses standard connectors. The low price is another argument, unfortunately slightly spoiled by the cost of the mini-crystal which is higher than the price of a normal crystal.

In order to avoid problems right from the beginning, the author secures the crystal with a bit of tape to the socket. Without this tape the crystal holder seems to be a bit weak.

Installed in a Parkflyer the XP8 FM shows an amazing range for safe flying. If more than 4 channels are required, 4 grams weight increase has to be accepted for the XN12 FM with 6 channels.

Becker Receiver SE 88

This unit produced by Horst Becker in limited quantity is the dream of most modellers intending to build and fly lightweight models. Definitely not cheap, the SE88 offers 2 servos and a 5 channel receiver in a box weighing just 18 grams. This is still unbeaten. Nevertheless the power of the two linear servos is just enough for small models. The SE 88 should not be installed in fast Parkflyers or models weighing more than 300 grams.

WES Technik JMP RX 5.23

Now we are coming to the very light and very exclusive parts looking at the JMP RX 5.23 receiver from WES Technik. At the time of writing this receiver is the smallest and lightest on the market. Biggest part of the unit is the

The Becker SE 88 receiver set in a model.

Parkflyers in Colour

The Pico Cub, once in the Air the power supplied by the Speed 280 is more than sufficient. This photo shows the open battery hatch in the bottom of the plane.

Above: The small Suchoj with the profile fuselage looks good from short distance although the design was made with a felt pen. Once in the air, she is as agile as the original plane. Below: The Parkflyer with an aerobatic layout is ready for a furious race.

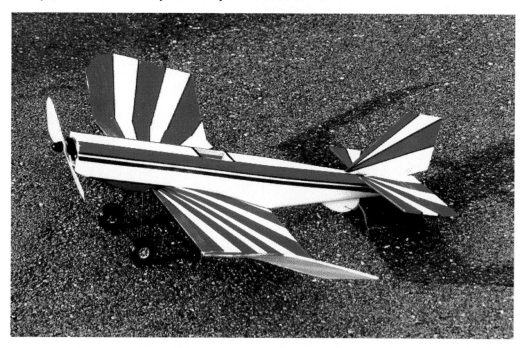

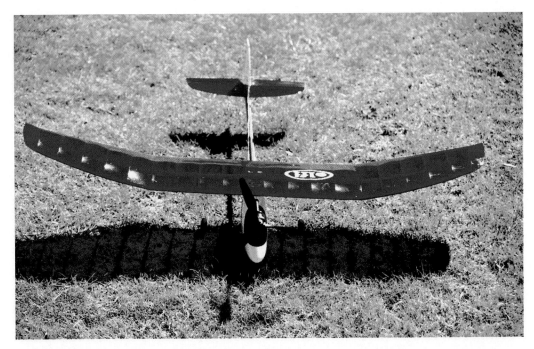

Above: The wing of the Elfi has a transparent film covering. Due to the wing section and the covering she can handle wind much better than other Parkflyers. Below: The Pou du Salle by IMA has a simple colour scheme but nevertheless she is a real eyecatcher on the ground as well as in the air. .

Above: The Extra 300 S Parkflyer by Simprop is nearly a fully grown aerobatic model handling most manoeuvres easily, as long as the pilot knows how to fly them. Below: This simple Parkflyer has a symmetrical wing section for aerobatics in small areas. With a geared Speed 280 BB there in more than enough power for most manoeuvres.

Left: The Tintanic Airlines Leo is one of the cheapest Parkflyers available as a kit in the marketplace. It is an interesting mixture of different materials such as wood, carbon fibre tube and Depron. Below: The Robbe Lo 100 looks good on the ground but in the air the view could hardly be bettered. She is a temptation for every real pilot.

Above: Is there anything more to be said about the Robbe Lo 100....Below: Flying low over the fields, the forests and the lawns. This is what the original Cmelak was designed for and it is big fun to do the same with the model.

Above: On the ground the thickness of the wing and the three blade propeller responsible for the thrust are dominant. Below: The Multiplex Pico Cub is ready for takeoff from the paved runway. Due to the small direct drive propeller starting from grass is very difficult.

With big wheels and the long landing gear, the Storch has no problem taking off from the lawn. Due to the qualities of the landing gear, the lawn doesn't have to be in top condition either!.

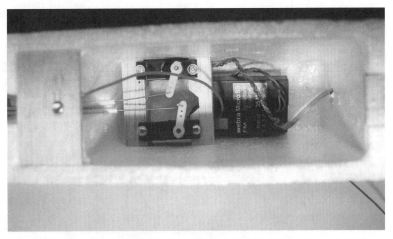

The Webra S 6 receiver seems to be old but works well in the Pico with plenty of room to spare.

plug section for the first five channels and most interesting is maybe the antenna with the diameter of a thick hair.

The receiving range is smaller than with most other receivers reviewed, but sufficient for small models, but it is questionable, whether the weight saving justifies the price of this small piece of art. You can buy two XP8 receivers at the price of one JMP RX 5.23. Maybe this receiver is better for the lightest indoor models.

Light receivers with full range.

If there is something like a good compromise, then these receivers are something for those Pilots who are not sure whether or not to start Parkflying. On one hand they are light enough to be suitable for a Parkflyer, on the other hand they have proven, that they are able to control a model also at the full range of normal R/C flying. And the best comes now, there is no premium to pay for the best of both worlds.

Simprop Pico 2000

With handy dimensions and a weight of under 20 grams this receiver is ideal for models with small or narrow fuselages and the Pico 2000 can easily replace any bigger and heavier receiver.

Even under Parkflying conditions other transmitters on neighbouring channels did not cause any interference. Full control of the model was guaranteed at all times during flight tests.

Multiplex Pico 4/5

This receiver too has shown that it is not only suitable for Parkflyers, but also for fully grown 10 cell hotliners and with such a model, the range of flying is definitely stretched to the limits. A receiver that works under these conditions perfectly, won't fail in close-up flying with a Parkflyer.

Webra Nano S6

With the S6 receiver Webra continues a good tradition in small receivers. So it is not surprising at all, that this receiver has given perfect service under all conditions of electric flying in Parkflyers as well as in other bigger electric models.

Multiplex "The Brick"

Just like the Becker Receiver/Servo unit the "Brick" from Multiplex is a unit consisting of a receiver and two servos. This reduces the amount of cables in the fuselage to the absolute minimum.

But the brick has not been designed for the needs of Parkflyers and therefore it is rather big. With a weight of 73 grams it also carries a lot of excess weight and is only suitable for rather big Parkflyers. But wherever

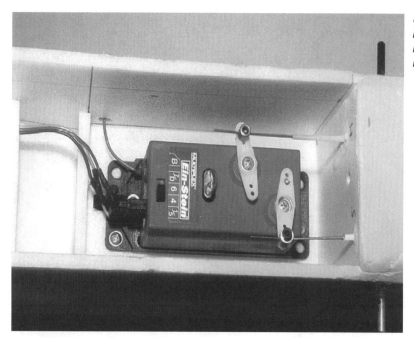

Unfortunately a bit big and heavy for a Parkflyer, the Multiplex Brick.

a Speed 400 pulls the model forward, the "Brick" is an alternative.

This shortlist of receivers is definitely far from complete, it mentions just those receivers in practical application in the author's hangar. As mentioned before, every receiver under about 20 grams of weight is suitable for a Parkflyer and, more important, I have not seen any really bad receiver on the market for a long time.

Servos

Six grams or nine grams? The situation with servos is easier than with receivers. On one hand there is a huge number of different types in the market, but at the bottom line, most of them come from the same source in the Far East. Trying to list all the different brand names and types, as well as copying the technical data from the catalogue sheets is rather useless and boring. Therefore please find a short distinction of the servos only by the weight.

In the 6 gram class most suppliers state, that the weight of the servo is only 5,6 g, which is true, if the cable and the connectors are cut off. As servos do not work without a cable and a connector to the receiver, the final weight ends up around 6-6,5 grams.

For a real Parkflyer, a 6 gram servo is definitely strong enough to swing the control surfaces, regardless of the label on the servo. Even slow Speed 400 Models won't need stronger servos, unless we are looking at aerobatic flyers with huge ailerons or elevators. They require 9 gram servos, maybe not for moving the ailerons, but due to the additional strength of the gearbox. Only if we are looking at 3D Aerobatic models, the power of the servos becomes important. In such models the difference between for example a Simprop SES 85 Servo with 0,85 kg/cm and a SES120 BB pulling 1,2 kg/cm with only 1 gram more weight becomes evident.

The 9gram servos are of course bigger and stronger than their tiny brothers. A Speed 400 aerobatic model needs the additional force as well as the more robust gearbox.

In both classes, servos with and without

A 6 gram servo has sufficient power to operate the variable incidence wing of the Pou de Salle.

ball bearings on the output shaft of the gearbox can be found. The additional precision will never do any harm to the model but it is doubtful whether it will ever be needed and the surcharge be justified. A Parkflyer probably does not require this type of precision and quality.

Of course bigger servos can also be used in a Parkflyer, but their weight will have negative influence on the flying properties of the model and the additional grams are just dead weight on the plane, that should be avoided. On the other hand smaller and lighter servos with a weight of just 2,4 grams can be found in the WES Technik catalogue, but these tiny units have barely enough power for a 300 gram Parkflyer and should be reserved for the smallest among the slow flyers only.

Control linkages

As important, as the servo itself is the connection between the control surface and servo. Ideally this connection is as short and as straight as possible, because then the connection is not overloading the servo and has no free play. Generally most Parkflyers can accept a bit of play more than big or fast models but it should be avoided in any case. Control surfaces that do not follow the servo exactly will reduce the precision in flying and in the same way the fun of flying. Some Parkflyers seem to have bad flying habits until the controls have been checked and improved.

The best thing of course is a short push rod from the servo to the control surface. Carbon Rods of 1,5 or 2 mm diameter are ideal, but a hard balsa rod will do the same job. If it has to be a "snake", inner tubes with about 1,2 mm diameter are sufficient together with steel wires of 0,5-0,8 mm. If the tube has to be bent, 0,8 mm is too thick in many case, but 0,6 mm wire will work fine and the tolerance is still acceptable. Least weight and zero free play can be achieved with Nylon wires in a closed loop configuration.

The control horns again have to be home made especially for a Parkflyer as most horns have holes that are too big for the connection

Short pushrods with no free movement are the answer for a good aerobatic flyer.

wire we shall be using. The best materials for control horns are 1mm sheet ABS or plywood or thin aluminium . The material from printed circuit boards is also very popular.

Motor controllers

The controller for the motor in a Parkflyer is more important than widely estimated. Controlling the propeller rpm in a Parkflyer is more essential than in most other types of electric flying models. Flying electric in many cases means, that the plane is started at full power and stays at full power until it has reached flying altitude where the motor is switched off for gliding. In a Parkflyer though, the ESC takes over a part of the elevator function. The speed of the plane as well as the sinking rate is controlled with the motor rather than with the elevator.

It is very satisfying to fly a model with just one or two clicks on the throttle stick. One step up and the model starts to climb without gaining speed and vice versa. For this kind of flying the controller must be able to follow the stick movement precisely and also be able to survive long periods of half power. Most speed controllers fulfil these two requirements without a problem at all, as long as they are not fighting with motors consuming the maximum allowed current.

Most ESC's designed for Parkflyers can handle about 5 Amps continuously which gives a sufficient safety margin for all Speed 280 applications. For a Speed 280BB they are just within the limit, if the motor is not driven to its limits by using too big propellers.

A Speed 300 is too thirsty for these controllers and should only be operated with a bigger controller to be on the safe side, a 10 Amp controller should be OK though. Same

applies to the Speed 400, but a suitable controller should be able to handle 10-15 Amps .

Unfortunately the manufacturers of the controllers are playing a confusing game concerning the weight of the units mentioning weights like 9 grams. Sometimes there is a short note besides stating "without cables", sometimes not. As electrical energy is not yet transmitted through the air to the motor, this information is confusing and the same ESC suddenly adds 5 grams to the weight of our new model once the connecting wires have

been added. It upsets sometimes, but at the end of the day there is nothing to be done about it but to ignore the catalogue information and calculate any speed controller at roughly 1 gram per Ampere of current it can handle. This rule of thumb normally works fine.

Rather important is also, how the controller reacts when the battery is nearly flat. All modern ESC's monitor the battery voltage in order to switch off the motor if the voltage is getting too low to supply the receiver and servos. But there are different ways for a

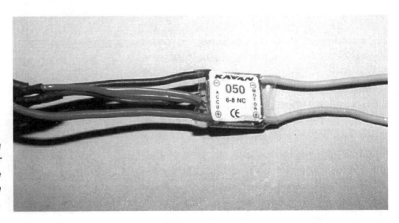

The Kavan 050 is a typical speed controller for Parkflyers. Tiny size is dwarfed by the connecting wires.

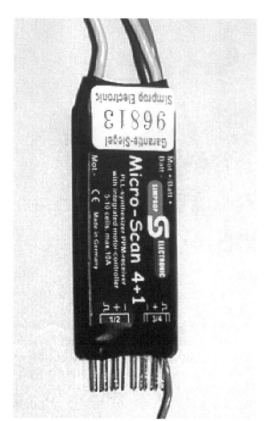

The Simprop Micro Scan 4+1 receiver incorporates a speed controller.

receiver to react.

Flying long periods with half throttle may prevent the Pilot from noticing the voltage going down and once the ESC cuts the motors at 2 meters flying level at the wrong place, landing can turn into a problem. Better, if the controller indicates that he will soon be forced to switch off the motor by turning the revs up and down several times before cutoff. Taking this signal seriously, the Pilot has got a fair chance to prepare for landing in due time.

The brake is another point to look at. Most controllers do not have a short circuit brake for the motor to force the propeller to come to a standstill. The turning propeller is no obstacle and braking is never good for the gearbox anyway. One the other hand, a windmilling propeller reduces the gliding properties of most Parkflyers to zero, which is not nice for landing without motor power.

A nice gimmick can be found on the Micro 5 BI controller produced by Heino Jung. Originally designed for Zeppelins, this controller is able to turn the motor in both directions. Later we will see, what can be done with the help of this controller. It is installed in the model Elfi.

Presenting individual controllers at this point is rather unnecessary, as experience has shown that the usual ESC's that can be obtained from the usual suppliers fulfil the requirement of Parkflyers very well and without causing problems. The Pilot just has to make sure, that the battery is connected with the right polarity and the controller must not be overloaded, although experience has

This picture shows the Kontronik Rondo Drive with the speed controller directly soldered to the motor.

Popular Jeti receiver is not the smallest around, modest price demands consideration for the larger Parkflyer.

shown, that even the 5 Amp controllers can handle 7 Amps for a short time. Nevertheless it is recommended to use a 10 Amp controller. The weight difference of 2-5 grams will not do much harm to the mode.

Upon installation of the ESC in the model, a place should be selected where the cables can be as short as possible and a bit of cooling air is also good for the controller, especially if full amperage is used. It is also recommended to separate the motor wiring from the cables to the receiver in order to avoid unnecessary disturbances of the radio equipment.

CHAPTER EIGHT

Parkflyers Reviewed

After so much theoretical background, it's time to start looking at real models trying to find out, for what kind of Parkflying they are designed and suitable. Please do not expect complete reviews of the models with an evaluation of the contents of kit, a description of the construction phase and a long flying report. This is what you find in model magazines on a regular basis.

Instead we will be looking at models that the author has actually built and flown and these models shall be presented here in a short and informative manner. This also means, that only the interesting and significant points of a model will be addressed. Furthermore it is intended to draw conclusions, if possible, from one model regarding a class of models as represented by the example reviewed. In this way it should be possible to get an overview, especially as a very wide variety of models has been chosen.

Parkflyers without own propulsion

As mentioned before, models without a motor are not typical for the Parkflyer scene at the time of writing these words. However, I see some modellers from the hand launch glider scene getting upset if their models are mentioned in this book at all. Small gliders, regardless of whether they are a mini-HLG (Hand Launched Glider) with up to 1 metre wingspan, or a "normal" competition HLG or an unlimited class model, are all suitable for flying on the neighbourhood football field or in the park. They are in particularly good company on a sports field, as flying an HLG really is sport in the true sense of the word and any reader that has the opportunity to follow a HLG competition will respect the physical performance as much as the flying skills of the Pilots. Sometimes I feel we should be ashamed to put a battery in our model and stay at one place controlling our model aircraft.

However, the topic of small HLG gliders would actually fill a book in itself, we shall only take a look at one model to see whether it can be flown under Parkflying conditions and from that we can draw the necessary conclusions.

Graupner Pitty

The Pitty by Graupner stands first in our line of models, as it is not really a Parkflyer, as mentioned before. The model is designed and built like a normal glider with a wingspan of

A small beauty; even on the ground. The Robbe Lo 100.

117cm less than the maximum for competition HLGs.

Pitty is built with a normal wooden construction with a rectangular fuselage from balsawood with a wing designed from balsa ribs, pine spars and partial sheeting made from 1,5 mm balsa. This method of construction has proven throughout the years that it is light but strong and can be repaired easily. Two properties that cannot be rated highly enough. Another positive point is the fact that the people at Graupner have been friendly enough to build the model completely and cover it with transparent film. There is a price to this

A look under the canopy of the Pitty shows the electronics compartment with the Sanyo Twicell 750 receiver battery for long flights.

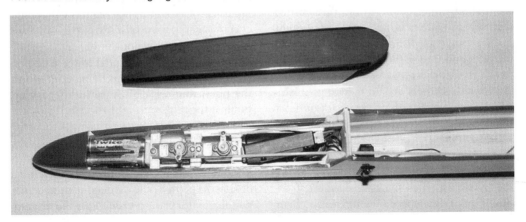

friendliness, but the quality of work justifies the price. It needs a very critical modeller to find real weak points.

The fuselage was designed by Graupner to accept even big servos and receivers without a problem. This keeps the costs low as Pitty can be equipped even with the cheapest servos and an old receiver that is too big for a Parkflyer. Due to the conventional set-up of the tail feathers, even simple transmitters without mixers can be used. All these points qualify Pitty as a nearly ideal model for the introduction into gliding. The final assembly of the model can easily be completed within 2-3 hours and there are no hidden problems. The building instructions are clear but nearly unnecessary for an experienced modeller.

Flying HLGs has something puritan about it, it is the most minimalist of R/C activities. No chargers, no batteries, just a screwdriver and the transmitter, that is all we need for flying plus a bit of free space . for throwing , flying

and landing. The Pitty can be flown from a big lawn in the park, or even better, a football field, without players is absolutely ideal. And there we are amongst sportsmen and will soon find out that model flying can be real sport. Throwing and flying, with a lot of flights in an hour or so is rather better exercise than walking or jogging, especially if the Pilot does not succeed in finding thermals to stay up long. Fighting for every foot of height is a challenge, even for enthusiastic electric flyers and leads to a kind of healthy addiction.

It takes less effort, if the model is launched with the help of a bungee. It reduces the physical effort to the picking up of the bungee for the next flight and stretching the rubber again. Pitty has proven that this kind of flying does not mean any stress for the structure of the model. The 6 gram servos installed at first seemed to be at their limit during the launch phase when the bungee was pulling so they were exchanged for 9 gram

Is there anything more to be said about the Robbe Lo 100….

types in the meantime and the problems vanished. The additional weight was welcome, the 10 grams of lead needed in the nose was removed. The resulting 320 grams of flying weight is not outstandingly low, but still acceptable. and due to huge 26,5 dm sq of wing area, the resulting wing loading of 12 g/dm sq is again in the midfield for Parkflyers.

The flying speed is higher than with a typical Parkflyer; we can blame this on the SELIG 3021 wing profile which is famous for excellent gliding performance and so a bit of room is required for a good landing. Nevertheless, half a football field is more than enough, even for a bungee launch.

Chosing this method of starting the Pilot should always keep in mind that the glider is accelerated to quite a high speed at the start. The Pilot must make sure, that no other person is endangered by the model on release.

The Pitty from Graupner is a very pleasant mini-HLG forming a good alternative to regular Parkflyers and can be flown with a lot of fun even outside dedicated model flying fields. A Pitty is not sensitive to wind at all, it can be flown in windy conditions, where other Parkflyers have to stay in the car. Another argument, that should not be forgotten.

Technical data:

Wingspan	117 cm
Length	925 mm
Weight	320 grams
Wing area	26,5 dm sq
Wing load	12 g/dm sq
Wing section	Selig 3021 modified

Robbe LO 100

Talking about the original LO100 as a glider for aerobatics seems unnecessary, as the full-size dominated aerobatic glider completions for years being without any serious rivals. The modern aerobatic gliders like the Fox or Swift only stepped onto the scene and took over, when the LO100 was nearly historic.

This legendary original motivated Robbe to launch the LO100 as a purely gliding Parkflyer. Thinking about methods to bring the LO100 to height, they also introduced the Fieseler Storch at the same time. Their suggestion is to aero-tow the LO100, preferably with the Storch, or with any other Parkflyer. This combination increases the fun factor of Parkflying, as two Pilots have to co-operate in towing.

The author first saw this combination for the in 2001 during an indoor meeting where towing seemed to be a little bit hectic and from the ceiling level of the hall the LO100 was just able to fly two circuits before landing. Not too exiting at that time.

But before we return to this point, let us take a closer look at the model. Similar to the other Parkflyers in the Robbe range, the LO100 is built completely from Depron. The kit contains the ready-made fuselage as well as a one-piece wing that is reinforced with a spar and two sheeting strips under and above the spar. This way the LO100 has a double-t shape reinforcement in the middle of the wing that ensures the rigidity of the wing.

A former near the nose of the wing and a balsa servo holder have to be glued into the fuselage and the tail feathers, from Depron, are glued to the end of the fuselage within a few minutes. The push rods for the control surfaces are included in the kit and are already formed. This means, that the LO100 is ready for flying within a few hours work. The building instructions are clear enough for beginners and due to the fact that the painting job is also done in the factory the finishing works are limited to attaching the stickers.

The secret of the LO100 is the coupling for the tow line in the nose of the model that allows a tug to pull the plane to height. The coupling is connected to the elevator servo in a way, that "full-up" will release the towline and the glide is started. Furthermore, there is a hook at the bottom of the plane for a bungee or a winch.

On a bright and sunny day with only little southerly wind my flying friend would let me rest until the little glider was airborne. A few soft hand launches were used for trimming, but it was soon clear that this is not the way to launch the LO100. With a weight of only 130 grams, made up of the airframe, 2, 6 gram

servos, a small receiver and 4 110 mAh cells for the receiver there is not enough mass to be accelerated in the starting phase. Apart from that the under cambered wing profile is only designed to produce lift at low speed.

In order to get a good flying height, a tug was wanted, as the Fieseler Storch was not yet ready built. A friend had a slightly overpowered Ikarus Taube ready for take-off and this was the solution. 6 or 7 metres of thin nylon cord was taped with one end to the Taube and the loop on the other end was attached to the tow hook of the LO100.

Due to the grass a lift off from the ground was not possible, but a hand launch of both models worked fine. The first turn proved the lack of aerotow experience of both. It soon turned out, that this starting method needs a lot of practice and it became clear why indoor flying was so hectic, but don't worry, it's fun to learn. At 50 metres height the LO100 was released and demonstrated that it is a nice glider. Later flights also showed that, even if there is no detectable wind at ground level, there might be more wind than expected at gliding level and the lightweight model with the extremely low wing load has a problem to fly against the wind.

On the other hand, there is a lot that can be done from 50 metres height and there is a good chance to find thermals that can lift this featherweight. Apart from the tow start the LO100 was also tested from a bungee launch, but the bungee must not be too strong for the tiny model. 5 metres of 5x1 mm rubber plus 50 metres of thinnest nylon cord produce enough pull to bend the wings of the LO100 without breaking them. With this set-up, 30 metres of height can be reached easily which is already a good basis to search thermal lift and reach several minutes of flying time.

The LO100 has a high degree of manoeuvrability and is able to fly in very narrow room and avoid trees, bushes and other obstacles if it is getting tight. If a

Waiting for the aerotow; the Robbe Fieseler Storch.

football field is sufficient for the Pitty, the penalty area is big enough for the LO100 apart from a bit of room for the bungee. The mechanical stability of the LO100 is more than sufficient. Without too much mass, there is barely anything that breaks in case of an accident. A vertical impact from 10 metres (receiver batteries can be empty at the end of the day) didn't do much more damage than a crumpled nose. Not good to look at, but it doesn't do any harm to the flying properties at all. With enough energy in the battery normal landings are no problem at all. The LO100 is that slow, that it is easy to control and catching the model in the hand is not difficult.

As a matter of fact, the LO100 has caused a change in the authors mind regarding Parkflyers without their own propulsion. This little darling has a lot of fun designed in, and even if the LO100 is not just a high performance glider, it awakens the ambition of the Pilot and what else are you looking for?

Such a small glider with a coupling for aerotows is an exception and the Pilot will soon discover that this is fun. I hope to see more Parkfly-gliders soon. This would increase the fun and there is hardly a cheaper model with less risk in flying to boot.

Technical data

Wingspan	98 cm
Length	640 mm
Weight	130 grams
Wing area	12,9 dm sq
Wing load	10 g/dm sq
Wing section	undercambered plate

Motorised gliders

After we have found out, that pure gliders are very suitable for Parkflying it seems logical to check motorised gliders. A small motor to bring the glider to a certain flight level is much more comfortable than throwing the model or rigging up for a bungee start.

Unlike the classical Parkflyer the motorised glider will only use the motor power

to reach a flight level that allows it to search for thermal lift with the motor switched off and the propeller folded to the fuselage. For this reason the usual under cambered flat plates are not the ideal wing section for a performance glider, as they cause too much drag at raised speed. This means, that different building techniques are required for the motorised glider as well as for the pure glider and we have to find out, whether the additional weight of motor and battery will have a negative influence on the ability to land on limited space.

Graupner Terry

This name sounds familiar to many older modellers that remember the small power model for 0,8 cc Cox motor under this name. Such a model sure is not a Parkflyer at all, but since 2000 a small electric glider with the same name can be found in the Graupner catalogue completely made from moulded Styrofoam.

With a wingspan of 1005 mm, the Terry is rather a small model with the looks of a shrunk hotline glider. In contrast to its looks, Terry is a two-axis (rudder/elevator) controlled electric glider with a wing loading of around 25 g/dm sq. So, rather a softie.

According to the catalogue the wing profile is RG14, which again is frequently used for hotliners and promises a wide speed-range. This impression is assisted by the Speed 400 direct-drive motor with the small folding propeller. The flight tests will have to prove how much room is required to land this plane.

The moulded wing comes out of the carton in one piece, which means, that we have a rather small model, but a huge carton, which is already equipped with a handle. A good idea, as the ready built model can be transported in this carton too, when wing and horizontal stabiliser are taken off. There is also enough room for a charger, batteries and the transmitter in the carton. The complete model flying equipment can be transported this way on a bike or even on a bus or train to the flying field. An advantage for all those who are not in the position to drive their own car.

Opening the box we find the wing, moulded fuselage, and the tail. In addition

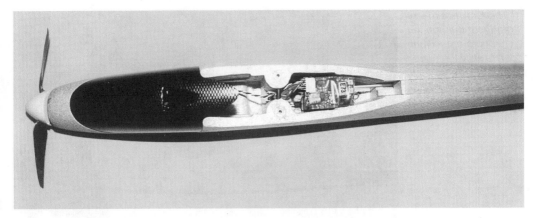

Terry unveiled - the R/C equipment fills the space available, battery is in the nose.

there is a punched plywood sheet, cabin cover, decals and a bag with small parts for the completion of the model. Not too much, but all that is required to finish a Terry in just one afternoon.

Before the gluing starts, all Styrofoam parts should be sanded with fine paper to remove the little blemishes and edges that are inevitable in production. Doing it carefully takes half an hour, but it pays at the end of the day. While all the other jobs can easily be done in the living room , this work should be completed outdoors as a bit of dust is involved.

There are different ways of gluing. The hasty ones, amongst whom the writer can be found, will use foam-friendly cyano, the more patient modellers will use white glue or epoxy. Before the former No. 4 is glued in place, it's better to check whether the battery will fit through the opening; it is easier to widen the opening at this stage than later. The pine spar that strengthens the tail end of the fuselage can be glued in with cyano, but the vertical fin, that also closes the channel for the pushrods should be glued with white glue in order to have time for adjustments. The turned aluminium socket for the wing screws and the stabiliser is custom made making sure that both parts always sit in the right place. The

other accessories are also at the top end of the market quality wise. Just what we are used to seeing from Graupner.

The complete assembly is described in the big plan sheet and there are no problems occurring at all. With the help of cyano the model can be ready in 2 hours, especially as the huge decals help the Terry to live without painting. Before assembly of the electronics the weight of the Terry is 232 grams including 12 grams for the decals.

Using equipment that was in stock, the electronics of my Terry are a bit too big and heavy. The Speed 400 with a separate ESC has about 10 grams of excess weight compared to the motor and ESC unit proposed by Graupner and the Robbe RS 500 servos are also too big and too heavy. The Graupner C261 servos would have fitted in place without additional work, while the slots had to be widened for the RS 500's but this is not the fault of Graupner at all.

Further weight comes from the 8 cell battery available compared to the 6 cells Graupner proposes. The final weighing brought a result of 545 g which still is alright in the author's view, although Graupner is indicating a top weight of 520 grams. Let us wait for the flight testing to see the effects of 25 grams overweight, 5% of the total weight.

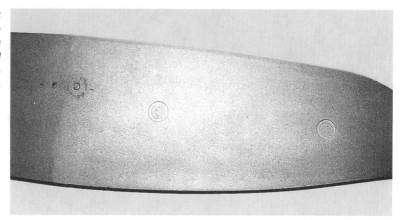

The prominent marks from the mould on the bottom of the wing don't really look good but they do not have any negative effect on flight.

In case of difficulties it is still possible to reduce the weight by reducing the number of cells.

Unfortunately weather was not as perfect for a maiden flight as the building instructions would propose but in December frost has to expected anyway. Obviously the Terry did not seem to be very impressed by the circumstances. After an easy hand launch, the model climbed steadily into the cold but blue skies, just like a model with hundreds of flights already performed. The installed Speed 400/7,2V felt comfortable with 8 cells and the propeller proposed for the Terry and the climb is nearly as good as most hotliners. Cutting off the motor at about 100 metres altitude it soon became clear, that the Terry is not even slow in the glide and the model easily penetrates light and medium winds.

The RG 14 wing section guarantees that the model does not only look like a hotliner, it also flies the same way. First concerns regarding the weight and the stability of the wings are soon wiped out. In fast and tight turns or in windy conditions the wings do bow from time to time but they only bend and do not break at all. The number of test flights has confirmed the wings are tougher than expected.

Even a bit more wind won't do any harm and when other Parkflyers have to stay at home, the Terry is the first choice. Due to the low wing loading, the model lacks a bit of dynamics but the manoeuvrability of the model, even without ailerons, is absolutely sufficient. Ailerons are only missed, when aerobatics are on the program.

Landing the Terry, the good gliding properties and good aerodynamics strike back. Either landings are steep and fast or slow and stretched, but then the room required for the final approach is much bigger than for other Parkflyers. Nevertheless with enough room landings are generally easy and the point of touchdown can be adjusted by the Pilot with the elevator. Due to the lack of a landing gear, the Terry prefers a lawn for landing rather than paved ground or frozen ground as in the case of the maiden flight. This causes deep scars on the bottom side of the fuselage that can be reduced by taping the underside.

Handling the model is easy and fast. The batteries change through the canopy within seconds and the model is rigged very quickly on the flying field. This way the Terry is a good companion that can stay in the car for just a quick flight where there are fifteen minutes of spare time. The Styrofoam construction has a big advantage in summertime, as the model can also stay in a hot car, as there is no film that becomes slack in the heat. Due to this fact, the Terry has

The Graupner Terry flies like a small hotliner.

spent nearly a whole summer in the authors' car and got a lot of flight practice this way.

Conclusion

The Terry is an untypical Parkflyer with abilities beyond other models and one that is also fascinating to those modellers who didn't want to fly a Parkflyer at all. The fact that the Terry could be flown in wind conditions, where the fun with other Parkflyers has already ended and flying seemed to be impossible was extremely pleasant. This advantage has to be balanced against the fact, that the Terry needs more room for landing than slower models, but anyway a football field was big enough for safe flying.

Technical data

Wingspan	1005 mm
Length	810 mm
Weight	545 grams
Wing area	20,8 dm sq
Wing loading	26,2 g/dm sq
Wing section	RG 14
Motor	Speed 400 7,2 V
Battery	8 x Sanyo N500 AR

Graupner Tipsy

Parkflyer or electric glider or both? This is the first question that arises when looking at this Graupner model. A bit more than 300 grams of weight and a direct drive Speed 280 normally indicates a Parkflyer, but the foldable propeller and the lack of a landing gear signal that the designers had a glider in mind too. But the combination of both is tempting too and the Tipsy is worthwhile anyway. In addition to this, the Tipsy has an interesting look with the pusher propeller and the wing sitting on a pylon above the fuselage. Pusher propellers are supposed to have a better efficiency as they do not cause any drag on the fuselage and it will be interesting to see how the aerodynamics of the model work out in flight.

Taking a first glance at the parts in the kit, the Tipsy seems to be the smaller sister of the Terry reviewed above as she is made from the same grey material. In this case the wing is again moulded from one piece and the triple V shape gives the model an

The bottom of the fuselage of this Tipsy has suffered a bit from frozen ground.

interesting look. Especially as there is a lot of dihedral given by the designers which means that the Tipsy will have very stable flying properties. The stabilisers as well as the fuselage and the canopy are again made from the same grey foam which means, that there is a lot of surface to be sanded in order to remove the sharp edges from production. Leaving them on the surface would probably not harm the flight performance but it is a minimal effort done for the looks. The quality of the foam parts though is absolutely acceptable without any shrinkage or warps. The building instruction advises not to paint the model, as colours may attack the structure of the foam and cause weaknesses in the material. What a pity, but most modellers will be able to live with the design given by the decals. It is also a shame, that the balsa rod reinforcing the tail of the fuselage is located in the middle of the back and is therefore permanently visible, but anyhow, the Tipsy is not really a designer piece anyway!

With the help of cyano, but the foam-friendly version please, and 5 minute epoxy,

the assembly of the model is completed in a short time. Servos and control linkages are also installed without effort and within half an hour. Same applies for the installation of the Speed 280 motor and the speed controller on the wing pylon. Typical of Graupner, a big drawing as well as the instructions can be found on a big plan sheet answering question that might occur and giving tips for completion.

Building of the Tipsy is nearly as fast as reading these lines and if all R/C components are ready available, the model will be completely assembled in about three hours including the time that the glue needs for drying. This might be a proposal for the Guinness Book of Records!

Unfortunately this did not apply to the test model as there was one component missing, the specially designed folding pusher propeller necessary was supplied in a tractor version and it seemed to be impossible to obtain the pusher blades. But "impatience" is my second name and so the Tipsy had to perform her maiden flight with a modified

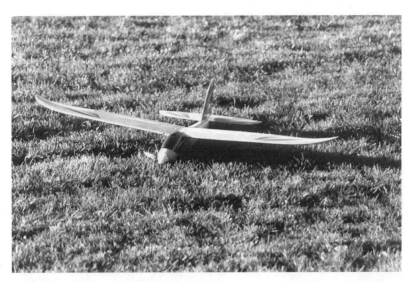

Günther propeller that was shortened until the blades would not cut into the fuselage any more. In order to attach the propeller safely to the motor shaft the black spinner was removed and the white blades were then fixed onto an aluminium adapter.

In order to bring the CG to the proposed position, the available 8 cell battery of Sanyo 700 AAA cells had to be brought to the most forward position, which meant, that some foam had to be removed. Otherwise the canopy would not sit in place.

Checking the weight, the scale showed 20 grams overweight clearly caused by the two additional cells, but the wings should be able to handle this.

The small sister of Terry is named Tipsy.

When wing and canopy are removed the complete electronics are freely accessible.

Hand launches with the motor running is easy. Just a bit of push is needed and the Tipsy is flying smoothly and steadily, as if the model has had years of flying practice. With the 8 cell battery there is more than sufficient power and the climb is of that kind that gives a lot of security even in turbulent conditions. After two minutes of powered flight it is time to switch the motor off and look for thermal lift. It does not make sense to climb much longer as a model with only 90 cm of wingspan soon reaches the limit of visibility. The result of the search though is absolutely positive. If thermals are available, the Tipsy will find them and due to the low weight is able to use them too. If there is nothing, even the best model in the world can't find anything.

The manoeuvrability of the model is very good, due to the big dihedral. The rudder works at any time and tight turns are easy. Tight turns are also the recipe for bringing the model back to earth when the search for thermals is too successful. Even without any reinforcements the foam wing can stand quite a lot. Even simple aerobatics like a looping or a stall turn is possible, but of course the light model will not maintain the speed desired for aerobatics. For gliding it is absolutely recommended to use the ESC proposed in the parts list, as most 5 Amp ESC's do not have a brake that stops the propeller from freewheeling. If the propeller does not stop, the blades do not and the subsequent drag destroys the glide.

It is not amazing at all, that a model with such harmless flying habit can also be landed with no problem at all. Due to the design with the propeller at the top, even landing in the hand is fun.

As Graupner proposed 6 cells only, this version also had to be tested, even if the author was a bit sceptical. The lower weight of the 6 cell pack had to be compensated for with some lead in the nose. Even now the climb rate is sufficient and definitely not a fight to reach height. With usual flying and no obvious thermal lift, the 700 mAh cells are sufficient for 24 minutes of flying. This is an excellent result but the sound created by the pusher propeller turning at high rpm directly behind the wing is not that nice. This creates a noise quite similar to a mosquito that is a bit annoying. What a shame, as a direct drive normally is very silent due to the lack of noise coming from the gearbox. But this is the only real point of criticism that can be found on the Tipsy that is well thought out in all other aspects, especially in respect of

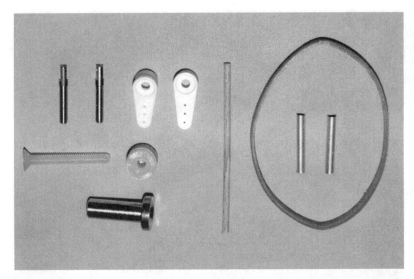

There are a few accessories required, but the kit is complete.

motorization. There is nothing cheaper than a Speed 280 direct drive and with 6 cells only, even the costs for a charger are low.

Technical data

Wingspan	888 mm
Length	740 mm
Weight	320 grams
Wing area	13,8 dm sq
Wing load	23,2 g / dm sq
Wing section	Eppler 64
Motor	Speed 280
Battery	6 x Sanyo 700 mAh

Simple Parkflyers

So what is a simple Parkflyer? You are right to ask this question, as this term has been used several times before. Simple Parkflyers in the eyes of the author are models controlled via Elevator and Rudder only that are designed for smooth flying in calm conditions. The control via two axes presupposes that both the model and Pilot do not intend to fly aerobatics apart from some basic figures. Relaxed flying is actually the focus for such models. Does that sound boring? Not at all,

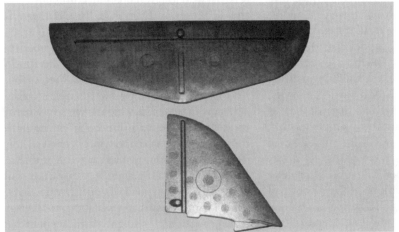

The stabilisers come out of the kit just like this.

The Pico Cub can also be flown indoors, if the reflexes of the pilot allow.

the challenge lies in the flying location with the possibilities for take-off and landing and handling the model in flight in these places. Most Parkflyers the author has flown so far, can be sorted into the category of simple Parkflyers, but I never encountered a lack of fun in flying these models.

Especially with these slow and manoeuvrable models it is possible to fly extremely low and circle around bushes, trees or street lamps and many challenges could be called "precision-flying". All this will not get stressful because the model is too fast or because just one tick on the throttle stick turns the model into a racer. All this fun in flying and the relaxation is a good part of what we are looking for in Parkflying. Because of this we should not disregard these simple models, but we should take them as a good introduction into this form of model flying. The Parkfly newcomer will soon learn, that controlling such a simple model in a confined area is not all that easy and he will be grateful for the time given by the low speed of the

model. Later, there is always the possibility to change to fast models with ailerons.

Multiplex Pico Cub

The Pico range of models by Multiplex comprises several small and simple models made from moulded Styrofoam that are targeting those modellers that do not want to spend so much money on models. The series started with the Smiley and continued with the Teddy, Twin Star, Pico Jet and then the Pico Cub.

The similarity in name with the legendary Piper Cub is not coincidence as the model looks rather like a Piper and the Pico Cub is also moulded from yellow foam the colour of many Pipers. The wings is known to many modellers as it comes directly from the same mould as the Teddy but in contrast to the Teddy the model now has a tractor propeller, landing gear and the wing is sitting on top of the fuselage.

The motor in the front of the fuselage pulling the model has a great advantage in that

Surely the similarity to a Piper Cub is not a matter of coincidence.

the propeller can now barely be heard. The Teddy was a good Parkflyer, but the pusher propeller was extremely loud and had an annoying sound which meant that trouble with the neighbours was programmed in as soon as I flew it in my garden.

The Pico Cub kit consists of the two wing halves, the stabilisers and the fuselage made from yellow foam and a vacuum formed cowling in yellow ABS. As everything is ready coloured, painting is not needed and the decals are sufficient to finish the design job. This shortens the time to take-off significantly.

Besides these big parts the carton contains

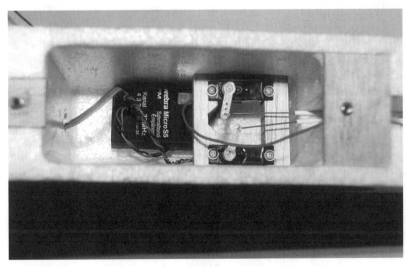

Plenty of room for the radio equipment.

a few die-cut plywood parts and a bag with all the small items required to complete the model. Even the motor, the propeller and the wheels are included. Only the radio components and the battery are still required.

The building instructions are in the form of a small booklet with 34 pages in 5 languages, which leaves about 5 pages for every language plus a chapter with pictures and sketches at the end of the book. Some parts are a bit complicated to read but with a bit of practice and with the help of the pictures there are no problems, especially as the Pico Cub is a very simple construction anyway.

The Styrofoam parts of the Pico Cub fit together very well and working with 5 minute epoxy the model is ready for installation after about two hours. The inside of the fuselage is big enough to accept the "Brick" but smaller 6 gram servos and a not so small receiver also find plenty of room under the wing. The assembly of the Speed 400 motor is quite basic, it is glued in, but this works fine and after another hour of relaxed working all components are installed and the control surfaces and the motor move properly. With 6 Sanyo N500 AR cells the model is slightly tail-heavy, but with 7 cells, the CG is just right.

As the grass on the model field was in a typical autumn condition, takeoff was impossible and the Pico Cub was hand launched by a friend for the maiden flight. Just a slight push was required, as the model didn't want to fly that fast anyway and after a few seconds of climb it was obvious, that the Speed 400/6V supplies enough power and that it can be throttled down significantly for level flight.

The model feels comfortable in the new element and behaves bravely without demanding too much from the Pilot at all, just like the original. Despite the missing ailerons the model is very responsive and can be flown on less than a football field easily.

It is amazing how well the small Günther propeller on the shaft of the Speed 400 harmonises with the slow flying model. Especially convincing is the low engine noise, rather caused by the propeller than by the motor. This was also appreciated by fellow model flyers watching the maiden flight.

They were finally convinced noticing the fact that the 500 mAh cells are sufficient for 9 minutes of comfortable flying with changing throttle positions and with the last bit of capacity in the batteries, the landing was easy too. Calculating from the long flight time the average draw of the motor must be around 3-4 Amps. This means, that the Sanyo 1850 cells in AA format would be ideal. Due to the higher internal resistance of these batteries 7 cells should be the minimum. The 60 gram increase in battery weight puts the CG a bit in front of the proposed position. With this battery flying time climbs to over 25 minutes flying the Pico Cub in the usual Parkflyer manner close to the ground with just as much throttle as needed. I can tell you, that this causes rather cold fingers in November!

In order to get the fingers warm again flying indoors was tried too in a big school gym. The Pico Cub could be flown, but suddenly the model seemed to be rather fast and needs a lot of practice and concentration.

Despite the small direct driven propeller, there was no wish at all to change to a geared motor with more power, as the direct drive provided enough performance for normal flying. Only in the rare case of a takeoff from tarmac with no wind, the Günther propeller has a struggle to produce enough thrust in the first moments and the model accelerates quite slowly. A takeoff from a grass runway is, due to the small wheels, impossible. The landing gear made from piano wire is very forgiving even in case of a rough landing and if the legs are bent, they can be repaired easily by hand.

All in all, the Multiplex Pico Cub is a nice

The Jodel BeBe really is a nice Parkflyer.

Parkflyer that provides a lot of fun without too much effort in building and without to much money involved. Together with the NiMh batteries the Pico Cub is very interesting for those Pilots that are looking for plenty of stick time from a single charge.

Technical data

Wingspan:	116 cm
Length:	780 mm
Weight:	520 -580 grams
Wing area	28,5 dm sq
Wing loading	18,3 – 20,3 g/dm sq
Motor	Speed 400 6Volt
Battery	6 x Sanyo N500 AR
	7 x Sanyo 1850 mAh

FVK Jodel Bebe

Looking at the technical data, the Jodel Bebe from FVK is a real Parkflyer, even if the construction is different to most other Parkflyers. The model is not designed from light balsa or Depron, but the kit contains a lightweight, white fuselage made from Epoxy laminate and a wing with a spar and rib construction that is already covered with heat-shrink film. The wing has a section similar to Clark Y with a flat underside and is fully covered like the wings of "normal" models. The tail surfaces and the control surfaces are made from 2 mm balsa and are also covered with the same film. A regular electric model for Speed 600 or bigger would be designed the same way, but stronger and the question arises, whether this construction is not too heavy for a Parkflyer.

At second glance, you can see, that the model was designed with scales close to hand. The fuselage is made from very thin layers of flass and resin and only the most important sections are carefully reinforced. The wings and tail feathers are built with the same care and the weight is absolutely acceptable. The same applies to the accessories included in the kit and the drive train supplied. It is a Speed 280 with a 4:1 gearbox and a light 3-blade propeller. The gearbox as such looks very similar to the ones from Robbe and Simprop and seem to come from the same source, but this does not have to be a disadvantage.

The assembly of the Jodel Bebe is smooth and fast as all parts fit perfectly. The servos are fixed with double sided foam sticky pads to the sides of the fuselage and there is plenty of room for the receiver. As the former for the motor is already glued in with the right angles, the installation of the motor is done in a few seconds. Connecting the ESC and the receiver with the servos and bending the control wires to the right length are the final steps before the Jodel Bebe is ready.

On the outside the final steps are the positioning of the decals, the gluing of the windshield and finally attaching the Pilot to the cockpit. All this takes less than 30 minutes but adds a lot to the looks of the model. A worthwhile investment! The 40 mm light wheels do allow the takeoff only from a firm runway, but , although the model is a low-wing-model, hand launching is easy and straightforward. The fuselage can be held with three fingers behind the wing and only on windy days, additional support under the wing is required to make sure the launch is straight.

Once in the air, the Jodel Bebe is as gentle as can be, but due to the wing section with less drag, a bit faster than other models. The geared Speed 280 has no problem at all in providing enough propeller rpm for typical Parkflying and with 8 350 mAh cells, 8 minutes of flying are the norm. Eight Sanyo 750mAh cells are sufficient for about 15 minutes but with little reserves for climbing. Despite the gearbox the model noise level is absolutely acceptable and the model has a breathtaking appearance flown at low speed on a calm day.

The higher speed potential of the Jodel Bebe turns out to be an advantage on more windy days, when other Parkflyers have to stay at home, because they would not be able to succeed against the wind and fly backwards. On such days the Jodel Bebe still moves forward and the complete construction is strong enough to withstand any turbulence. On the other hand the Jodel Bebe needs a bit more room for the final approach than a slower model with under cambered profile having the advantage of acceptable gliding properties so that landings can also be done without motor. The glide is nearly as good as with a small glider and the model is controllable at all stages of flight. Nevertheless she behaves well also when flown at minimum Speed. Although the surface of the wings is very smooth, the stall never comes as a surprise, but it is clearly visible when the model is flown too slow. Simple aerobatics with loops and stall turns are possible.

The Jodel Bebe by FVK proves, that it is also possible to design a Parkflyer with "conventional" construction methods, as long as the weight is kept under careful control. With a higher speed level caused by the conventional wing section, the model finds its own place in the hierarchy of Parkflyers allowing to fly in windier conditions, although all other technical features are absolutely Parkflyer. As long as the space for flying and landing is not extremely tight, the Jodel Bebe is ideal and ability to fight wind is definitely one of the big plusses for this model.

Technical data

Wingspan	100 cm
Length	720 mm
Weight	450 grams
Wing area	18 dm sq
Wing load	25 g/dm sq
Motor	Speed 280 with 4:1 reduction
Battery	8 x Sanyo 350 mAh
	6 x Sanyo 700 mAh

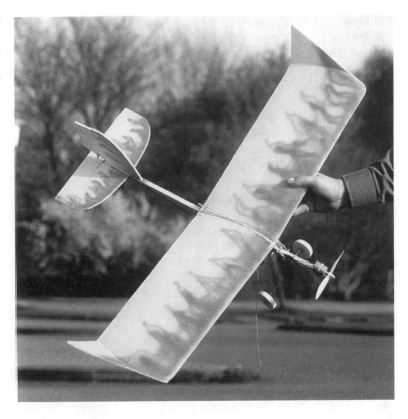

Truly a "hot" Parkflyer as far as the design goes but with the big indoor wing, the Liteflyer flies really slowly even outdoors.

IMA Liteflyer

The Belgian manufacturer Innovative Model Association (IMA), supplies under the name Liteflyer a Parkflyer such as we remember from the first days of slow flight. A simple model, where the fuselage consists of a balsa stick not even trying to look like an aeroplane.

Only at a second glance can differences be noticed as the wings are quite special. The wings of the Liteflyer are cut with a hot wire from Styrofoam just like the cores of model aircraft wings have been made for a long time. But in this case the wings are not sheeted with balsa, but they are hollowed. This reduces the weight by another few grams and the strength comes from a vertical balsa spar of only 1,5 mm thickness. The internal shape of the wing is cut so that the spar automatically sits in the right place. A bit of white glue added to the spar before insertion assures that everything

sits perfectly.

Due to the hollowing the wing has a thickness of about 3mm on the top as well as on the bottom , but this is still strong enough for normal use. The Styrofoam used is quite coarse textured and so the surface of the wing is not smooth either. This could be sanded, but the rough structure is positive, as it reduces the stall speed of the model again. It is also interesting, that the kit includes 4 wing halves. The two smaller ones are destined for the outdoor version of the Liteflyer and the two bigger ones can be used for the indoor version. This reduces the wing load and also the flying speed of the model significantly.

The wings are completed within a short time and the fuselage as well as the stabilisers are no problem either. The fuselage from a 10x10 mm balsa strip carries all the radio

equipment and the propulsion components. The wing sits on a small pylon and is held with rubber bands stolen from my wife's kitchen drawer. Rubber bands are also used to hold the landing gear and the stabilisers in place, making sure, that these items can give way if necessary. This is helpful if the landing is not all that perfect or when the car is a bit too small.

The motor sits in a carbon fibre mount and is fixed in place by - of course, rubber bands. The retention again is strong enough to prevent the motor moving in flight, but in case of contact with firm elements the propeller and the motor have the possibility to move.

Only the radio equipment, i.e. the servos, the receiver and the ESC are firmly attached to the fuselage. The control surfaces are connected to the servo arms with the carbon rods included in the kit. Without painting, the Liteflyer is ready for takeoff within two evenings of relaxed work, if the gluing is done with cyano.

For the first flights, the absolute Low-Budget propulsion should be tested. A direct drive Speed 280 with the well known Günther Propeller is normally the wrong thing, as the fast turning propeller does not correspond with the slow flying model, but all components were at hand and so it was an easy decision to go this way.

On a paved runway, 20-30 metres roll are required for takeoff with 7 350 mAh cells but then the model climbs steadily, just as if it has not done anything else before. Soon an altitude is reached where the motor power can be reduced and then the capacity of the cells is sufficient for 5-6 Minutes of flying.

Flying the Liteflyer is absolutely unspectacular, the model behaves as gently as can be and as gently as expected. The direct drive makes the model a bit faster than necessary and the Liteflyer cannot be hung on the propeller for climbing. But on the other hand this propulsion set is absolutely inaudible which is appreciated by sensible neighbours.

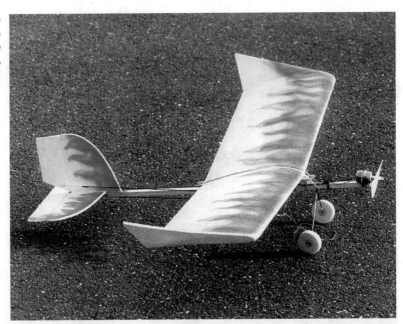

The airbrushed flame design is a nice contrast to the flying properties of the Liteflyer.

Currently my Liteflyer is used a flying test bed, especially on the battery side. As the battery is located at the CG with enough room around it, different shapes and different weights of tested batteries can be tried without influence on the CG.

The smallest battery so far tried was 6x110 mAh Sanyo cells, still sufficient for 3-4 minutes of flying time and the biggest were 8 cells 750 mAh keeping the model up in the air for up to 13 minutes.

The two different wings both have their places. The smaller wing helps the Liteflyer to penetrate wind more easily and the big area of the indoor wing is first choice when there is barely any wind and the model can be flown at lowest speed and in tight locations. The direct drive has shown so many good properties, that a geared drive has not been missed at all and the installation has never happened. The non-existent noise from the motor is simply marvellous and anybody being disturbed by the direct-drive-Liteflyer is more than sensitive.

The excellent slow flying properties of the IMA Liteflyer with the indoor wing and the inaudible propulsion set turn the model into an ideal Parkflyer in the true sense of the word. Due to the good flying properties the model is also very good for the entry into Parkflying.

Technical data

Wingspan outdoor version	70 cm
Wingspan indoor version	80 cm
Length	750 mm
Weight outdoor	235-250 grams
Weight indoor	250-290 grams
Wing area outdoor	15,4 dm sq
Wing area indoor	19,4 dm sq
Wing loading outdoor	15,2-16,3 g/dm sq
Wing loading indoor	12,7-14,9 g/dm sq
Motor	Speed 280 direct
Batteries	6-8 cells 110-750 mAh

Elfi

You don't know Elfi? What a shame! Elfi is a Parkflyer from the same source in the Czech republic as the Jodel Bebe and the Cmelak,

Elfi really looks a bit strange, but in flight Elfi is a perfect model.

with excellent flying habits although her looks are a bit unusual. Elfi doesn't follow the usual construction schemes for Parkflyers. The front of the fuselage is GRP moulding and the tail is a carbon tube. The wings are a spar and rib construction covered with semi-transparent film. So, a bit different, but as the Jodel has proven, it can work and we shall see how Elfi flies finally.

Before the maiden flight, Elfi needs to be rigged and completed but the manufacturer has already done most of the work so that very little remains for the modeller, but many of us are grateful for this. The wing is ready built and covered in a professional quality, that most average modellers would not reach after a long practice. Even the holes for the fixing screws are prepared and only a small dowel has to be installed to make sure that the wing does not twist. The stabilisers from 2 mm balsa are also covered and the control surfaces

are hinged with tape. Horizontal and vertical stabilisers just need to be glued together at a 90 degree angle.

A bit more work has to be done with the fuselage. The tail tube and the motor holder are already glued in and the tube is machined to accept the prepared tail feathers. The geared Speed 280 is also installed and wired. The gearbox is of good quality with a brass pinion on the motor and a brass tube functioning as a bearing for the bell. This is more precise than plastic bearings on the shaft and the gearbox, as well as the three bladed propeller, are very silent in flight.

The landing gear wires are all pre-formed in the factory and can be installed within a few moments. Installing the radio control components is no problem either. The snake outers are attached with tape to the tail boom and the servos are held with double sided foam sticky pads on the sides of the fuselage.

Cutting the piano wires to length and connection of motor, ESC and servos to the receiver are the finishing jobs. The battery is held with Velcro tape.

3-4 hours are enough for a competent modeller to finish the Elfi, if necessary on the living room table watching TV as no dirt will be produced at all. The building instructions are rather short but they don't leave any open questions. The CG is mentioned as well as the proposed throws of the control surfaces.

Like the Liteflyer, Elfi can accept different types of batteries as the battery is located at the CG and the weight of the batteries does not affect the balance of the model. The manufacturer recommends 6-7 cells and the model was tested with capacities ranging from 110 mAh (very light) to 700 mAh (NiMh for long flights).

The initial flight of Elfi happened to be in a big school gym, independent from the weather conditions outside. 360 grams of weight and the flush surface of the wing are quite a lot for indoors but the flight turned out to be successful anyway due to the size of the gym.

The landing gear with three wheels guarantees that the model tracks in a straight line and Elfi is airborne after 10 metres. Once in the air, the motor rpm can be reduced immediately as the geared motor supplies plenty of power. As the motor is running at reduced power most of the time 7-8 minutes of flying time from a 350 mAh pack is normal. Landing on the wheels shows that there is only little rolling resistance and the model rolls and rolls.

A few days later the weather improved and Elfi was allowed to fly under the sun. Again the takeoff from paved ground was easy and the model lifted off, more or less without the interference of the Pilot. Once trimmed properly the little aircraft climbs steadily and the model reaches cruising altitude without any correction from the Pilot.

Outside the possible speed range of the models proves to be positive. The profiled wing would also suit a small glider and therefore Elfi flies steadily forward, when others are already in reverse gear. A 7 cell 250 mAh battery is quite sufficient, there is not even the desire for a stronger motor. Plenty of power for looping and stall turns is available and more aerobatics are not required from such a model. Installing 8x750 mAh cells Elfi stays airborne for up to 20 minutes even without the help of thermal lift.

The gliding properties of Elfi are only reduced, when the propeller is windmilling due to the lack of a brake in the ESC. If the ESC is equipped with a brake, Elfi could also be used as a motorised glider searching thermals on quiet evenings.

Once again the layout of the model dictates that the landing approach is not as steep as with some other models and therefore a bit of room is required to finish a proper landing. Due to the good landing gear Elfi also rolls a long way, especially if the runway is slightly sloping. Based on the author's laziness the idea came up to stop Elfi with reverse thrust by using the Micro 5 BI bi-directional ESC from Heino Jung, which allows the propeller to turn in both directions. As a matter of precaution, the forward direction is controlled through the complete travel of the throttle stick while the reverse can only be used with the sliding channel of the transmitter. This is to make sure that reverse is not applied, when the throttle is taken down in haste. When the model now touches down and reverse is applied, it comes to a standstill after about 2 metres. Amazing plus the sound of the propeller turning in reverse, that intensifies the impression of a turboprop plane that is braking with reverse pitch of the propellers. In the air, this function has to be used carefully, but landing approaches can get very steep, with just a bit of reverse carefully applied. Nevertheless the motor should be in idle just before touching the ground.

With or without reverse thrust, Elfi is a great Parkflyer supplied with an excellent drive train too. It will be difficult to find a better model/motor combination on the market of ARF models and the quality of the components of the kit is outstanding too. These points alone justify the price and the fun in flying comes as a bonus on top.

Technical data

Wingspan	100 cm
Length	750 mm
Weight	360 grams
Wing area	14,8 dm sq
Wind load	24,3 dm sq
Motor	Speed 280 with 4,33:1 gearbox and 3 blade prop
Batteries	6-8 cells 110-750 mAh

Leo by Titanic Airlines

If the kit for a radio controlled model costs about £20, even the meanest of modellers take notice and the temptation is almost irresistible. This train of thought makes the decision to purchase the Leo from Titanic Airlines easy.

But what can we expect from a model that cheap? The answer is found in the box. After opening there are the two dominant parts of the kit in the form of the wings halves. They are Styrofoam cores sheeted with light 1 mm balsa. The cores are already cut to the correct root angle, so that the dihedral of the wing is accurately set.

The front section of the fuselage is built from CNC milled balsa and plywood parts that are interlocking, so that the fuselage builds with no effort and with little chance to make a mistake. The only advice that can be given is to sand the parts before assembly, then they fit together much better. The rear part of the fuselage is a carbon tube with a 5 mm outside diametre. The stabilisers are made from 6 mm Depron, only the nose of the horizontal stabiliser is made from a balsa spar that is glued to the Depron within seconds. Furthermore the kit contains a few milled plywood pieces like the firewall and the control horn as well as a steel axle for the landing gear and the pushrods.

Despite the low price the kit is absolutely complete. The only missing parts are the rubber bands to hold down the wing and the wheels which is acceptable considering the

Motor installation as it should be and without the risk of overheating.

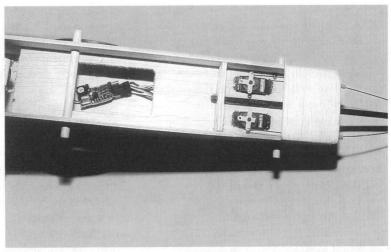

The Leo has sufficient room for the radio equipment. The small components used are not an absolute requirement.

price of the model. The instructions are complete and understandable so that there should be no problem in completing the model even without a lot of building experience.

The finish of the Leo is of course a matter of taste, the only point is avoid making the surface of the wing too smooth. A bit of roughness is welcome to reduce the minimum speed. My model was only treated with clear filler to protect the wooden surfaces against humidity. Same applies to the fuselage and the nose of the horizontal stabiliser.

Titanic Airlines proposes to use a Speed 400 with 3:1 gearbox for the model, but as I had a Simpro Fun drive 450 lying around unemployed and this drive set had already proven its quality, the decision was clear to use this system for the Leo, the only problem was posed by the huge 11 inch propeller reducing the ground clearance to a minimum even though large Ikarus wheels were installed. The motor is controlled by a Schulze 15 Amp ESC and two HITEC HS 55 Servos together with the Simprop Indoor 2000. Power supply is taken care of by 8 Sanyo N500 AR cells.

With this equipment the Leo weighs 585 grams and the wing loading is calculated as 33,4 g/dm sq; this results in rather fast flying

for a Parkflyer. This is assisted by the Eppler 205 profile with the flat underside. These profiles are generally faster than the typical under cambered Parkflyer profiles.

These expectations were confirmed in course of the maiden flight. While the gearbox remains nearly unheard, the model flies quite fast around the flying field. At full power the propulsion proves to be very adequate for the model and just one full circle is enough to reach a safe altitude where the rpm can be reduced. But even at 1/3 of the throttle travel, Leo remains pretty fast, but still a pleasant flyer.

After five minutes of cruising, there still is some capacity left in the battery but nevertheless it is prudent to make a first try for a landing. Even with the motor switched off completely the glidepath is acceptable and there is no need to keep the propeller turning for landing. This makes landings easier for inexperienced Pilots.

For the next flights, a 2mm balsa packing was fixed under the nose of the wing in order to increase the angle of attack and allow lower speed . This balsa piece has become a firm part of the model in the meantime, but the model is still relatively fast for a Parkflyer. The profile and the wing loading are responsible

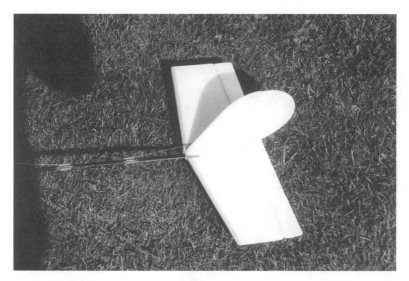

Opposite to the wing the stabilisers are made from 6 mm Depron.

for this. Despite the minimum ground clearance of the propeller, the model can take off even from a short lawn but finally one landing ruined the pinions of the gearbox. Consequently the Wasp drive Set from Modellbau Gross was installed instead. This is a Speed 280BB with a 5:1 reduction and a three blades 9 x9 in propeller. With the same 8 cell battery there is nearly the same power available as with the Speed 450 and it is also possible to use 350 mAh cells. This means a weight reduction of about 60 grams for the motor plus 60 grams for the battery so that the wing load goes down to 26,5 g/dm sq. This set-up rather looks like a Parkflyer. Now it is still possible to fly fast, but it is also possible to fly much slower than before. The 350 mAh cells are sufficient for five minutes of flying and the old N500 AR last at least 8 minutes.

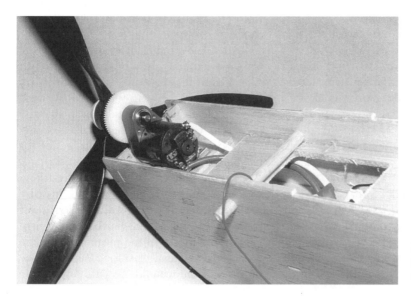

The Groß Wasp in a well ventilated working location.

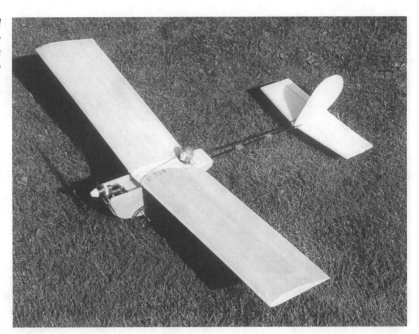

Wood, carbon and Depron are the characteristics materials of the Leo.

At an unbeatable price Titanic Airlines supplies a robust and fast Parkflyer that can not only be flown in calm conditions. Due to the speed the Leo is not just ideal for a narrow flying field but the obligatory football field is definitely big enough too. No matter whether the geared Speed 400 or the Speed 280 is installed, the fun is guaranteed with Leo when doing aerobatics at low altitudes.

Technical data

Wingspan	100 cm
Length	820 mm
Weight	585g/465 g
Wing area	17,5 dm sq
Wing loading	33,4/26,5 g/dm sq

Cmelak

"Bumble Bee" would be the translation of the Czech word Cmelak which is a proper description for the full-size agricultural flyer that has often been built as a flying model. Now there is also a kit in Parkflyer size with 100 cm wingspan of this model available to the market. The Cmelak kit is definitely up to the design and manufacturing standards we

have come to expect from Czech model designers. Using the word "kit" is even misleading as the carton of the model just contains two handfuls of parts that allow a modeller to build a complete model in just one afternoon. First of all we have a wing that is designed in conventional ribs and spars with a perfect yellow film covering. In contradiction to the instruction sheet the wing even has the ailerons ready connected with pushrods. The finishing work consist of the installation of the servo and gluing in the control horns. Furthermore the wires for the landing gear have to be attached. 30 minutes and these jobs are done, including a cup of tea in between.

Just like the wing, the stabilisers are ready covered and the control surfaces are hinged with clear tape. They are glued to the fuselage with Epoxy. A definite plus must be given to the fact that the covering of the horizontal stabiliser is already removed in the gluing area. The former that holds the motor under the cowling is also glued in, and the motor with the gearbox is already installed in the factory. Two balsa sheets can be found in the kit, that

Really nice and even quite scalelike; the Cmelak by FVK.

are glued into the fuselage for the servo mounts. The pushrods from 0,8 mm piano wire with the relative tubes together with the control horns for elevator and rudder are also included in this very complete kit. Only for the installation of the battery does the modeller have to find his own solution as it would not be a good idea to attach the battery with double sided sticky tape to the side of the Resin fuselage. My model has a battery box made from 1,5 mm sheet balsa that is held with a screw from the bottom of the model. A packing piece on the underside of the wing makes sure that the battery cannot move once the wing is fixed.

The motor included in the kit is again a simple Speed 280 and manufacturer has already wired and installed the complete unit. Only the three bladed propeller and the bell of the gearbox with the internal pinions must be mounted to complete the propulsion system.

Final touches to the model are in the form

of self adhesive decals for the letters on the side, the windows of the canopy and some little things. Although this is not very much, the Cmelak looks very nice and scale-like after this procedure. The fact that there is no transparent canopy, but only some silver stickers for the canopy windows does not do any harm to the looks of the Klemm.

The construction of the model was completed with a function test and the use of the scales, which brought a slight disappointment though. With 8 350 mAh cells 450 grams of all-up weight is quite a lot for the small Speed 280.

The conditions for the maiden flight were anything but perfect as the winds could not be called calm at all. Nevertheless the Cmelak started from the tarmac of the car park after a short roll. After a few moments it became clear that the Speed 280 propulsion set did not have any problems coping with the weight of the model and the throttle stick could be

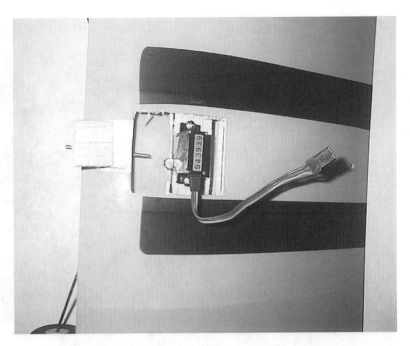

The servo for the ailerons.

reduced for level flight. Half power is sufficient for relaxed cruising, although the flying speed is still significant. Again the wing load and the profile make sure that the model is travelling from one end of the tarmac to the other quite fast. But on the other hand this is helpful in windy conditions.

The fact that the Speed 280 handles the weight that easily might lead to the assumption, that the amperage in flight is rather high, but the flying times from 7-9 minutes with a 350 mAh pack show, that this is not the case either. Obviously the fine tuning between model, propeller and motors works well. Flying fast with high rpm, the landing has to be planned after about 7 minutes and for a 9 minute flight the throttle hand has to be quite sensitive, but nevertheless the result is better than average.

As the Cmelak is controlled via all three axes, the model is very responsive and prefers to be flown with all controls. Rudder and ailerons together produce the best turns, but the model can be flown with the rudder alone rather than with the ailerons alone. This observation becomes evident, knowing that there is also a Cmelak version without ailerons available that is a bit lighter, but otherwise shows the same positive habits. Unfortunately the power of the ailerons is not sufficient to perform rolls, but even simple aerobatics are a lot of fun with the Cmelak.

More than 50 flights have shown, that the model is very robust, only the wooden spar that holds the landing gear had to be fixed twice with a bit of cyano, but all other parts proved to be strong enough for rough handling. Only the propeller caused a bit of hassle, when one blade broke after a rough landing. Theoretically the blades can be exchanged individually but in this case the propeller and the bell of the gearbox are glued together and so the complete unit had to be thrown away. In order to continue test flying the bell of a Simprop gearbox and an APC 10x7 slow propeller took over. The flight performance remained more or less unchanged with this set-up.

Flying low over the fields, just like the original.

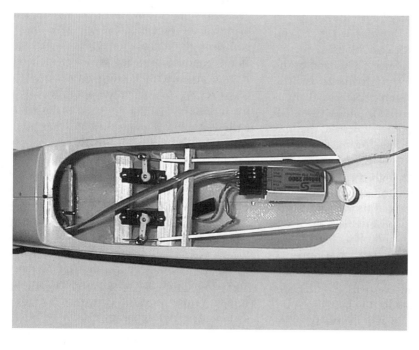

Plenty of room in the fuselage for servos and the receiver.

Apart from the accident with the propeller, top marks can be given to the manufacturers of the Cmelak kit. The quality of the components is close to perfect and all parts fit together without additional work. This way a fully grown Parkflyer can be built in the course of two evenings or just one long afternoon.

Once in the air, the weight of the model is soon forgotten and the power train, although very simple, is first class. Powerful, fast, silent but also effective. These attributes can be attributed to the motor/gearbox/propeller combo and it is not easy at all to achieve this combination. During my flying there was never any wish to modify.

It is not surprising that the Cmelak is not as slow as other models with an under cambered wing sections, but nevertheless the "Bumble Bee" handles well and can be flown in light wind also.

Technical data

Wingspan	100 cm
Length	700 mm
Weight	450 g
Wing area	16,7 dm sq
Wingload	27 g/dm sq
Motor	Speed 280 4:1 reduction
Battery	8 cells Sanyo 350 mAh
Propeller	Three blade 9x9in included

Robbe Fieseler Storch

If an original aircraft is already on the lines of a Parkflyer, then the model should be a good Parkflyer too. This is a possible train of thought whilst looking at the Fieseler Storch produced by Robbe. The original "Stork" was able to take off and land on a football field, an ability that pushed the development of helicopters into the background for some time.

The (Short Take-Off and Landing) STOL properties of the Storch were legendary although the designers had to use some tricks such as wing slots and spoilers to increase lift at low speeds. In addition the Storch had an extreme landing gear allowing touch downs on rough grounds or at minimum speed close to a stall. Characteristics we would like to have for our Parkflyers too.

The model has to perform without any aerodynamic aids on the wings for reasons of simplicity, but the flying properties of the Fieseler Storch are convincing. Although rumours were going round that the model needed modifications to fly properly, the plane was built without any modification.

The kit is designed following the typical concept of Parkflyer kits from Robbe and Simprop. The fuselage consists of two vacuum formed half shells of Depron that are already glued together. The stabilisers are made from 3 mm sheet Depron and the wings are made from 6mm Depron that is vacuum formed to the right profile. In addition to that, a few punched plywood parts are included for a spine for fuselage reinforcement and for the assembly of the interior. All visible parts are already painted. Furthermore pre-formed wire parts for the functional landing gear, wheels and clear plastic parts for the canopy as well as the control horns and wires are included. Robbe also includes the gearbox and the propeller, so that only a simple Speed 280 is missing for the power train. These add up to a tidy sum and we should keep this in mind when evaluating the price of the kit.

For completion only the radio equipment and the battery is required. Due to the high degree of pre-assembly in the factory the construction of the Fieseler Storch is an easy and fast job. All formers fit into the fuselage without a problem and can be fixed in place with foam friendly cyano. The wooden parts in the area of the canopy should be sanded and painted in black before assembly, as they remain visible though the big clear windows. Only a matter of appearance, but it adds a lot

The landing gear is a bit reminiscent of a Cranefly but it does a perfect job. .

to the model. These are the only paint jobs for the model, all other parts are already finished. Even the positions of the wires for the landing gear are marked, so that no error can be made here.

Before gluing the wings to the model, the motor as well as the radio equipment should be installed and tested, as the one-piece model becomes a handful and there is a good chance, that it will be damaged in the course of the installation. Finally the cutting and attachment of the wing struts is a tricky job demanding careful work, and a bit of experience is helpful, to get the wings onto the plane without any misalignment. Here the building instructions could be more exact giving the right length of the struts rather than leaving this to experiment. An error at this stage means distortion of the wings that has a serious effect on the flying characteristics of the Storch.

Here we have to work with great accuracy.

The centre fixings of the landing gear should be glued with Epoxy, as this section is quite stressed and the forces during landing should be transferred to the fuselage evenly. Otherwise the landing gear works perfectly and is absolutely forgiving just like the original.

The scale shows a final weight of 320 grams with an 8 cell 350 mAh pack. According to the building instructions the weight should be 280 grams with 6 or 7 cells, so the difference lies in the batteries which is acceptable and definitely within the limits. The Speed 280 with a 1:4,5 gearbox and the 9x6 slow fly propeller should be able to handle this. As the responsible deities also produced a calm Saturday morning, the maiden flight of the Fieseler Storch proceeded without any delay. The first flight with 8 cells showed that the Storch is well powered with this set-up. A short roll on the ground was followed by a steep climb straight to a comfortable altitude. The climb was steep, but not too steep as the model did not show any tendency to stall.

Despite all critical opinions the model flies with barely any corrections on the trims and is easily controllable. With the motor throttled down to about 25% the Fieseler Storch is really slow and can be used for precision flying around the street lamps. The model follows the rudder inputs without hesitation but is not over sensitive; the elevator though could do with a bit more throw than suggested in the instruction booklet, especially when it comes to landing.

But if the landing is not all that soft, it doesn't matter either. The landing gear is first class and absolutely scale. The 5cm of travel is outstanding in this class. The model looks a bit like a spider on long and thin legs, but again, this was typical for the original plane too and the softness helps with any kind of landing. Only the wheels made from two ABS half shells each are not that perfect. On paved ground they are noisy and they have a tendency to split on the glue line. Sooner or later they should be replaced by foam wheels.

After the maiden flight with 8 cells the Storch had to prove, that it can also perform with less power. With 7 cells the start from a paved runway is still good and in the air sufficient power is available. With 6 cells however, performance is marginal. The model needs about 50 meters of runway before lift-off, even from hard ground and the climb is close to the minimum. Most of the time the Storch has to be flown with full power that is reflected in the flying time. Eight 350 mAh cells are sufficient for 8 minutes of flying while 6 cells of the same capacity are flat after 5 minutes. Even a bigger propeller does not help in this case.

The power of the regular Speed 280, even with 8 cells, is not sufficient for an aerotow of the Robbe LO100. For this application the

The rear part of the cabin is reserved for the servos and the receiver.

catalogue proposes, absolutely correctly, to use a Speed 300/6Voly that will provide full performance with 6 or 7 cells.

Together with the Speed 300 and a 5:1 gearbox, an 8x4,7 propeller is the right choice to get the Storch flying. Six cells now are sufficient for normal flying, and with 7 cells the model just rolls about 5 meters on a grass runway before lift-off. With 8 cells, the model just jumps into the air before a nearly vertical climb. This is more than enough for aerotows

and with a bit of communication and practice between the Pilots, these are big fun. This power would also be nice for pulling a banner.

Robbe's Fieseler Storch definitely is a good flying Parkflyer with an interesting look, that provides a lot of fun to the Pilot at an acceptable cost. Despite the slightly raised wing loading compared to the light ones among the Parkflyers, the model is nice and slow and extremely manoeuvrable. Just like the original, that landing gear absorbs most of the loads coming from touchdown and turns landing into one of the favourite flying manoeuvres. Surely there are Parkflyers demanding less construction time, but with the Fieseler Storch every minute in the workshop is invested well and the look of the flying model is the pay back.

Technical data

Wingspan	105 cm
Length	670 mm
Weight	320 g
Wing area	19,4 sq dm
Wingloading	16,5 g/sq dm
Motor	Speed 280 4,5:1 reduction 9x6 Slowprop Speed 300 5:1 reduction 8x3,8 Slowprop
Battery:	6 – 8 Sanyo 350 mAh

The Robbe Fieseler Storch, even the original was more or less a manned Parkflyer:

Except for the antenna, this picture could also be taken for an original Storch.

Even on the ground the Pou du Salle is something special.

IMA Pou du Salle

There are some original planes, that tempt modellers to reproduce them as flying models time and again, even if the flying habits of the original were doubtful and it is not certain that the model will fly much better. The Pou due Ciel or Flying Flea might be called an ultralight from the early days of flying. She has two wings of nearly the same size, staggered in a unique way and had flying characteristics which could only be described as "marginal". Nevertheless modellers have always tried to prove that the Flea can fly and the Belgium company IMA has taken the risk of producing a full Styrofoam Parkflyer version of this plane, calling the model Pou du Salle or "Parlour Flea" roughly translated.

This idea cannot be ignored by a real model flyer and the author was tempted by the model for quite a long time before buying it.

The kit consists of of a few CNC cut Styrofoam parts and some pieces of wood as well as a complete drive set with a Mabuchi 050 with a gearbox attached. Both wings consist of three parts that already have the root angle cut to form a wing with dihedral on both sides of the straight centre section. Before gluing these parts together the surfaces should be sanded to the typical shape shown in the instruction.

Apropos of the instructions - there are no written instructions given with the kit but there is a CD with a very comprehensive 50 page building instruction manual with a lot of pictures in the English language that can be printed out.

While the wings are glued and drying, both halves of the fuselage can be glued together. Before gluing, it is a good idea to hollow the fuselage a bit further than shown in the instructions in order to gain more room for the radio equipment. The test model later needed some hollowing of the nose of the fuselage, as the battery had to be installed as far forward as possible to bring the centre of

Unfortunately the original Mabuchi 050 was not powerful enough for the model.

gravitiy to the right place.

Care is needed to glue the two vertical struts that hold the wing in place. These must be perpendicular to the longitudinal and lateral axes of the model. The two servos for the Pou are fixed to the side walls of the fuselage and they are supposed to control the rudder and the forward wing with the help of 2 mm steel wire pushrods. They were replaced by carbon rods of the same size in the test model. Nobody will ever be able to prove that this is necessary, but it is a good feeling to know that everything was done to keep the weight of the model low. Later the weight saving was compensated for by the colour that was sprayed on with foam friendly spray from Graupner on the wings and the fuselage. But this investment of 10 grams has added a lot to the appearance of the Pou du Salle and so I do not regret having done it.

With the regular motor, 8 110 mAh cells and the Multiplex ¾ Pico receiver the model comes to a final weight of 220 grams. Rather a lot for the Mabuchi 050 but we shall see.

Setting the right angle of attack for the front wing is a bit of a tricky job, as the changing of this angle is actually the elevator function of the Pou du Salle. The basic adjustment can be done as per the instructions, but there should be room for final tuning.

After angle of attack, CG and the control throws were adjusted roughly, there were no more excuses for putting off the maiden flight. The first flight was due to start with a take off from the ground, but the run ended after a few meters, as the propeller touched the ground and the main pinion was stripped instantly and could not be repaired.

For the next flight the Pusteblume unit from Gross was installed. This time a friend hand launched the model by running until he felt that there was enough lift to get the Pou airborne. The set-up of the front wing was proven correct with the trailing edge about 30 mm over the surface of the rear wing. The following successful flights confirmed the correctness of this position and the Pou du Salle slowly circled at about three metres height.

Unfortunately the power of the Mabuchi 050, is only just sufficient for level flight and slow cli mb of the model and the condition can barely be called "flying".

If a plane looks good on the ground, is also looks good in the air later.

Consequently the next modification was the installation of a S240 Slowfly propulsion set, again by Michael Gross. The increase weight of motor and gearbox was welcome, as the CG can now be achieved more easily and the battery does not have to sit in the most forward position anymore. Unfortunately the ground clearance of the model is extremely low and therefore the original wheels have been exchanged for wheels from the Robbe DR 2000 in the meantime. Now take off from paved runways is not a problem.

With this drive set flying is a real pleasure, at full throttle the model climbs safely and half power is still enough to keep the Pou du Salle in the air. The speed level of the model is really slow and the possible turning radiuses are minimal, just right for small flying areas. Unfortunately this light model does not really like wind and the wish for aerobatics does not even come up at all. I am sure, Claude the Pilot, (he just has to be there), wouldn't appreciate loops either. Slow circling close to

the ground at minimum speed is what this vintage plane just loves and here the model looks absolutely scale.

This is Parkflying at its best and it is a lot of fun to circle the mole hills on the lawn. In addition to that the Pou du Salle attracts a lot of attention, from spectators.

Thanks to the low wing load of about 10 g/sq dm the Pou du Salle is not only a good Parkflyer for calm conditions, it can also be flown indoors, even in smaller gyms, as the name says. So the winter season is safe too.

Technical data:

Wingspan front	73 cm
Wingspan rear	500 mm
Length	480 mm
Weight	220 g
Total wing area	21 dm sq
Wing load	10,5 g/dm sq
Motor	Gross S 240 Slow Fly with APC 9x6 Slowprop
Battery:	8 cells 110-150 mAh NiCd

Ready for take off. The fuselage of the Nomad is painted in red and yellow and the windows are marked with a felt pen.

Built from scratch - The Depron "Nomad"

The Australian TV programme "The Flying Doctors" is famous around the world and since the broadcasting of the programme, the Australian built aircraft "Nomad" is also known in Europe playing one of the major rolls in the series. It is a twin engine STOL (short take-off and landing) aircraft that has shown its qualities in the demanding service of the Royal Flying Doctor Service in the Australian outback. It is a simple construction twin engine, high wing aircraft with an almost rectangular fuselage section which is nearly ideal for a scratch built model. A few minor modifications though are required for the Parkflyer. An available three-view of the Nomad was enlarged on the photocopier to get a model with about 80 cm of wingspan. The fuselage was built from 3 mm Depron sheet but the scale thickness of the wings would have been 9 mm only and therefore much too small for a Parkflyer.. A rough

estimate of the likely final weight suggested that around 360 to 380 grams with two cheap motors and 8 350 mAh cells wpould be achievable. The desired wing loading ought to be around 20 g/sq dm which meant that about 18 sq dm of wing area would be required required. So the wingspan was increased to 1000 mm and the depth of the wing was doubled to 18 mm. The stabilisers were enlarged accordingly and soon the drawings for the Nomad were ready. Thanks to foam friendly cyano, the construction proceeded quite quickly and after about one week of building, the model stood on the 30 mm wheels ready to accept the motors and the radio equipment. As the model is only controlled by elevator and rudder, this job was also done in a short time and model was soon finished.

The two motors driving the Günther propellers are a bargain from an electronic shop at a price of less than 50 pence each. Unfortunately they are 2,4 Volt motors and

The fuselage has a huge volume of space for the batteries and R/C equipment.

even in series they take about 7 Amps from 8 cells. With this input, the Nomad races along the car park, but the leg of the nosewheel was too short, so that the model needed a lot of elevator for lift off. This problem has been overcome now as the nosewheel leg has been increased to a 35mm.

Once in the air it soon became obvious that the Nomad had too much power. At full throttle the model is a real racer, but if the power is reduced the appearance of the model becomes better and 7 Amps is too much current for the 350 mAh cells anyway. Flying at one third power, the small Nomad looks like the original as far as the speed is concerned and she stays airborne for about 8 minutes. Fast flying though will be punished with only 3 minutes of flying fun from one battery charge. The wing has a flat underside and therefore the Nomad is an acceptable glider despite the poor aerodynamics. Landings should be made with the assumption that there will be a long glidepath. The fixed nosewheel

that is not steerable is a help for take off, as the model cannot swing off line too easily, but it turns out to be a disadvantage after touchdown as the model rolls a long way without the facility to turn and taxi back. Therefore the Nomad would be another candidate for the "reverse thrust" controller such as fitted to the Elfi.

If no paved runway is available the Nomad can also be hand launched although landings on grass can bend the 0,8 mm piano wire nose leg quite a lot. The sound of the two propellers is just perfect, as only a low humming can be heard. Even one more Parkflyer in the air at the same time means that the motors of the Nomad cannot be heard any more. Therefore it is advisable to check the flight time also with a stopwatch in the transmitter to be sure that the controller does not force a landing by cutting the power supply.

Despite the significantly enlarged wing area, the looks of the model are still acceptable

With sufficient wing area, even modern planes can be flown as Parkflyers.

and only an expert will be able to tell the difference. This model proves, that it is also possible to reduce modern planes to Parkflyers as long as enough wing area is available so that the wing loading stays at an acceptable level. Compared with conventional electric flyers this Parkflyer still has the advantage of the lower wing loading allowing a lower speed level that looks more like the original.

Technical data

Wingspan	100 cm
Length	680 mm
Weight	380 g
Wing area	18 sqdm
Wingload	21,1 g/sqdm
Motors	2 Igarashi 2,4 V with direct drive Günther propellers
Battery	8 cells Sanyo 350 mAh

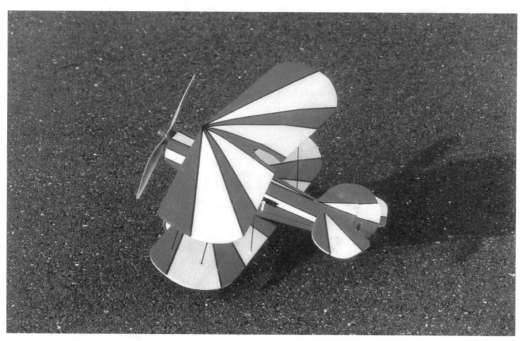

With a lot of power and 3 servos controlling all
axes this small Pitts is a lot of fun to fly.

*One of the first scratch-built aerobatic
Parkflyers completely made from Depron.*

CHAPTER NINE

Even More Fun in the Park

Many readers will have their own ideas as to the meaning of this headline, but in this book we should limit ourselves to model flying as this is the topic suggested by the title of the book. So, what can we do, if we feel bored by flying in circles around the molehills or checked the length of the lawn with the landing gear? Aerobatics could be one of the spontaneous answers to this question. They are always good to check the limits of ones own flying skills. Most Parkflyers are able to fly a loop that is more or less round and - not as easy as it sounds- a stall turn is also possible. But without ailerons such things as a roll or a cuban eight are barely possible. A bit more Power than available in the majority of "normal" Parkflyers would also be very welcome for aerobatics. Apart from that, the construction of the model should provide a bit more strength, so that the model will not disintegrate in flight.

For these reasons there is not really any alternative than to design special Parkflyers for aerobatics, that should be controlled via all three axes, that have sufficient power and that are indestructible in the air. At first sight, these three demands seem to be difficult to realise in a lightweight Parkflyer, but there are models around that prove the fact that it is

possibleand descriptions follow.

Another alternative means to increase the flying fun in the park would be pylon races with Parkflyers, although we have to keep the possible dangers in mind at any time. It is too much of a temptation to take a Speed 400 class racer to the park but these models definitely are too fast and should only be flown on designated model fields. At the end of this chapter you will find a proposal for a pylon Parkflying class that keeps the safety aspect under control too.

Nevertheless it is an error to believe, that Parkflying without aerobatics is boring. Even with a model controlled by rudder and elevator only it is possible to have a lot of fun and there is no need to look for a new model straightaway. Imagination will always help to find new challenges for a Pilot depending on the flying area.

As mentioned before, precision flying is one of the challenges. Two trees standing close to each other can be such a challenge and a lamppost can do the same job. A narrow footpath in the park is not that easy to approach for landing or touch-and-go's. Try it and you will find this a big enough challenge for the moment, it is not as easy as it seems to be. Same applies for precision landings on

La Drenalyn offers a lot of room for the imagination of designers.

narrow spots that are difficult to approach. Believe me, every flying area has such challenges with different degrees of difficulty. Is not really necessary to fly in a forest as a clubmate of the author does from time to time if he feels bored flying on the field in front of the forest.

For these manoeuvres a simple Parkflyer is definitely sufficient, but now we want to look at models that can do more.

La Drenalyn

Le Creuzot is a small town in Burgundy, in heart of France that barely any reader of this book will know. Why do I mention the name of this town then? Quite simple, Le Creuzot is the home of a traditional indoor flying meeting in France for which some inventive minds designed a really interesting model for indoor and outdoor flying. Playing with words, the plane was named La Drenalyn being a disc from 3 mm Depron of about 60 cm diameter with a Depron fuselage. With a powerful motor in the front of the fuselage and two control surfaces operated by strong servos

with huge throws this model guaranteed fun in the air.

Indeed the model is built nearly as quickly as you can read this following the plans that are available on the internet under www.lecreuzot.net/aeromodelisme. Even if you do not read French, it is no problem to build the model following the pictures and for the first model nobody will lose too much time being too eager to get this thing flying. Another plan of La Drenalyn is available on the net in German language under www.buschPiloten.de. Here you find further pictures to make the construction self-explanatory.

The wing is cut in one piece from a 3 mm Depron sheet and unlike the plans, the authors model has a full fuselage with 3 mm Depron sides and a bottom from 6 mm Depron. The shape of the fuselage sides dictates the profile of the wing. Some people would give the Drenalyn more profile than others in order to get more lift. If a powerful motor is planned, a shallower profile has proven to be better otherwise the model has to be flown with "down" elevator at high speeds. With "only" a geared Speed 280 the profile shown in the plan is fine.

For limitless flying fun, a bit more power is required. A Speed 280 with 8 350 mAh cells and a 4:1 reduction together with a 10x7 or 11x4,7 Slowprop is good for flying and maybe a loop. A roll needs more speed and hovering is only possible for a short amount of time.

With a Speed 300, 5:1 reduction and a 9x4,7 Slowprop, full throttle is only needed for a fraction of a second and vertical hovering needs less than full power allowing transition to vertical climb from this position as full throttle is applied. For the launch a model with this power set-up is no longer hand launched. It is enough to put the model vertically on the ground and with full power the model lifts of vertically. Depending on how many of these stunts are flown a 7 cell battery with 350 mAh will last 2-3 minutes only. With a Simprop Acro Drive 350+, a Speed 280BB with 5:1 reduction and a 9x6 propeller, the same power is available, but 1-2 minutes plus in flying time are possible compared to the Speed 300. This shows the true quality of the Speed 280BB. With a 10x4,7 propeller endless vertical climbs are possible with an 8 cell battery with a capacity of 350 mAh. Flying indoors, for which the Drenalyn was originally designed, this is only possible for a split second. But the model is also at home outdoors. The wing load is extremely low, but due to the powerful drive train, the model flies very well under all conditions.

The manoeuvrability of the model is outstanding. A volleyball field with just 9x18 metres is absolutely sufficient to try everything and have fun for a full battery load. 5 metres of open space are perfect for circling and the landing strip need only be as big as a towel as the Drenalyn can be flown with extreme angles of attack on half throttle barely moving forward. With a bit of practice these landings are absolutely easy.

The true Drenalyn junkies are still practising to achieve vertical landings with the model standing on its tail, but it can only be a matter of time before they will succeed. This is then the high art of Parkflying.

And if this is not enough, there is also the possibility of flying in a forest. Yes- IN- a forest between the trees and bushes. Once you have seen this, you know the model is agile.

And if one of these things fails the model can, thanks to the fully Depron construction, be repaired with a bit of cyano and activator within minutes. If the repair is not practical, even a new model is built within two or three hours. A regular sheet of Depron is sufficient for at least two models so that the cost of a new Drenalyn is acceptable too.

The big surface of the model temps one to play with the design of a colour scheme and if you don't like the design any more, just accept a bit more risks flying stunts and have a reason for a new Drenalyn. I am sure one Drenalyn will never stay alone for long and flying in a group of identical model definitely increases the fun anyway. Even dog fighting is possible and soon there will be slices of Depron in the air that's for sure!

If required, the Drenalyn can also be scaled down, the minimum is 40 cm so far for the author. This truly is a model for the drivers of small cars that want to carry the model in one piece though.

There is no other model cheaper or more simple that can give so much fun in and outdoors. But be careful, there is a great danger of becoming addicted to this drug but due to the price the addiction is not a critical state at all!

Technical data

Wingspan	60 cm
Length	660 mm
Weight	280 – 300 g
Wingload	8-10 g/sqdm
Motor	See text
Battery	See text

Looks like a big one: the Extra 300 S by Simprop.

Simprop Extra 300S

The Extra 300 S by Simprop is a model of the famous aerobatics plane and like the original is a plane optimized for this purpose. Like sister planes from the same Simprop range, the Suchoj SU31 and the Cap 231EX, the Extra is a Parkflyer that is not built to fly low speed circles a few metres above the ground.

These models are noticeable first of all by the pure volume of their fuselages and by the fact that the wings are made from two vacuum moulded half shells forming a symmetrical wing section. The "proper" wing profile also gives these models an advantage over simpler models with curved flat sheet wings. Furthermore they are equipped with big ailerons and there is no doubt that they have to be controlled via all three axes.

Besides the fuselage, the wings and elevator are all made from vacuum moulded Depron. The kit contains prefabricated

wooden parts for the formers, formed wires for the landing gear and a clear canopy with a Pilot that has to be glued from two ABS half shells just like the wheel spats.

All Depron parts are painted in a very light grey, even lighter than shown in the catalogues. Unfortunately they are very susceptible to dents and scratches. For this reason the building board should be clean and free of unnecessary stuff like screwdrivers etc. If possible a soft towel should cover the surface to be absolutely safe.

As usual the building instructions are very comprehensive and there are no tricky points whatsoever. An experienced modeller would be able to do without completely, but even these people should take a look from time to time. The most interesting idea in the design of the Extra is the way nearly all heavy components are located in the same place. The former at the leading edge of the wing holds the landing gear as well as the battery and also the front fixing for the wing. As long as this former is fixed properly into the model, nothing serious can happen.

Before the installation of the motor, the customer has to decide whether a conventional gearbox or one of the ball bearing Simprop AcroDrive 350+BB is going to be installed. In this case the firewall has to be bigger and is fixed a bit further towards the back of the model. In the model shown, the firewall sits in the forward position for the conventional Simprop gearboxes as this makes the exchange of drive combinations easier and with the variety of different reductions and motors available, it should be possible to find the perfect combo for the model.

As per instructions, the wings should be glued to the fuselage. As this turns the Extra into quite a bulky plane, the test model was built with a removable wing. A rubber band at the main former holds the wing and the bottom part of the fuselage make sure, the whole thing remains invisible.

The removable wing also allows the radio equipment to be installed through the wing cut-out rather than through the canopy opening. The prefrabicated pushrods and adjustable servo mounts are a standard in the Simprop kits that is very welcome. It makes the installation a matter of one or two hours. Looking at the weight of the model and the power available it was a good decision to refrain from 6 gram servos and using 9 gram servos instead. The additional weight can be justified in such a model.

Simprop has also done a lot for the appearance of the model, although the wheel covers and the original Pilot were not used. On one hand the author has to admit, that he does not like to build things from half shells, on the other hand the wheel covers won't last very long taking off and landing from a grass runway. As the big canopy would be empty without a Pilot, a foam dummy was glued in the cockpit. He looks as good as the original Pilot anyway.

Even the flying properties of this Parkflyer are similar to a bigger model.

In order to achieve a vibration-free propeller, the spinner has not been installed either as I could not get it to run true. Nevertheless the Extra looks good with the big stickers and maybe the spats will be used in winter when the grass is very short.

The first motor installed in the Extra is a Speed 300 with a 5:1 reduction and a 9x4,5 Slowprop as this set-up has shown a high top performance in the Drenalyn. The lower efficiency had to be accepted in this case. The maiden flight on the model field soon showed, that this propulsion provided good thrust . Starting from grass the model rolled about 10 metres to liftoff and the Extra climbs at a 45 degree angle constantly. Throttling down to about 1/3 power the model circles at level flight giving time for the Pilot to get used to the model. The Extra 330S is reacts fast to the input of the controls and due to the three axis control the model can be flown precisely. The angle of attack of the wing and the CG are adjusted as per instructions and they seem just right. Only a small bit of trimming is required. It seems that if the throw of the elevator is too big it is hard to fly a round loop. Obviously the throw causes a stall at the elevator. With less throw, the loops are bigger and round.

The power of the ailerons is sufficient. The model does not perform rolls in a split second but at a natural speed. The rudder is only required on the ground and for example for a stall turn. Flying inverted is no problem at all, only a bit of down elevator is required.

After about three minutes, it is time to think about landing if full power is only used carefully. The 350 mAh cells would only survive about 90 seconds of full power and even that should not be tried, if the cells are to last more than 20 flights. Full power should only be used for seconds, e.g. at the beginning of a loop or stall turn. This needs discipline but it's a good training though.

There is no reason at all to be afraid of landing. The approach to the landing should be flown with the last bit of battery as landings are smoother with the propeller turning and the landing gear will absorb the last bit of energy. As expected the Extra has a glidepath that awakens memories of a brick when the motor is cut off completely and the motor should be used to make landings better. But this bad glidepath can be used to reduce the required space for landing, as long as the motor is reactivated shortly before touchdown. This is an advantage in confined areas.

In flight the model seems to fly like a Speed 400 fun flyer rather than like a Parkflyer. Compared to a Parkflyer the Extra 330S can handle quite a lot of wind which extends the possibilities of the model significantly.

In aerobatic mode the model surprises with its versatility and the capability to fly all the standard manouevres. Most of the time the Pilot rather than the model sets the limit of aerobatics and the performance of the Speed 300 in this model is astonishingly good. This motor handles the Extra very well and the wish for a stronger motor does not really come up although the model would definitely do better with a small brushless motor and 10 cells 500 mAh. There is still some potential to be explored!

Technical data

Wingspan	89 cm
Length	770 mm
Weight	440 g
Wing area	20,6 dm sq
Wing loading	21,8 g/dm sq
Motor	Speed 300/6V
	5:1Reduction 9 x 4,7
	Slowprop
	Speed 280 BB 5: 1
	Reduction 10 x 4,7
	Slowprop
Battery:	8 x Sanyo 350 mAh

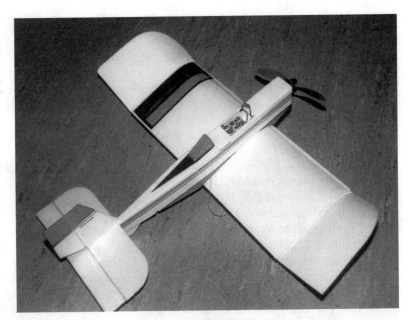

The first attempt to design a Park Pylon Racer. Did not last long as a result of an over-enthusiastic pilot!

Park Pylon Racing

Once man gets bored, he will look for new challenges. This way aerobatics were first invented and at nearly the same time people started flying circles around pylons to perform the first air races. It seems only natural, that Parkflyers are starting to think about pylon races sooner or later. But Parkflyers generally are rather slow and the fastest Parkflyer would be outpaced by any Speed 400 racer flying with half power. This definitely is not the sense of it, especially as these little Speed 400 bullets are too dangerous to be flown in populated areas and they are hard to see and to control anyway.

For this reason it needs some simple rules for pylon racers that are at the same time Parkflyers. In addition to that, it is widely understood that racing is a risky business with a lot of model losses. Therefore the models should stay simple and cheap. Furthermore an expensive cost battle on the motor side should be avoided. Together with some clubmates the author tried to set up a few simple rules for the models:

Rules for Park Pylon Racing

Mimimum weight	250 g
Max wing load	20 g/sqdm
Wing profile	under cambered plate
Landing gear	yes
Motor	Speed 280 or Speed 300 or equivelant
Minimum reduction	3:1
Battery	8 cells 350 mAh
Racing time	4 minutes

The minimum weight of 250 g can be achieved with a simple Depron model so that expensive construction with exotic materials is not required. A maximum weight is not required as the maximum wing loading would otherwise cause models to become too large.

The under cambered plate as wing section reduces the possible maximum speed and creates enough lift at the pylon. Apart from that, this type of wing is easy and fast to build. The landing gear is helpful for every day flying and reduces maximum speed again. The Speed 300 motor keeps cost down and with the right

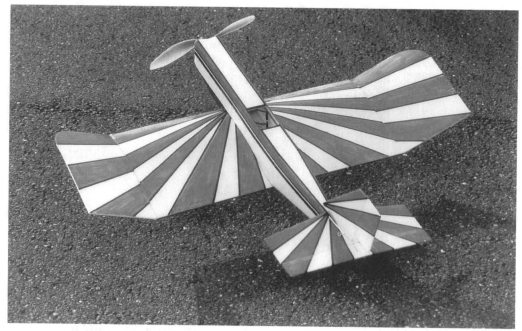

The second version doesn't look much different. Both models have proven that they are also very good for "normal" flying.

reduction has an acceptable efficiency in a fast model although the speed of a direct driven model will never be reached. With 8 cells and a model of 250-300 grams there is sufficient power available that needs to be controlled first of all.

Some readers may think that a model with these parameters can't be all that fast and that

pylon racing with such a plane is no fun. Try it first ! You will soon see that it needs a lot of practice and concentration to fly a model like this under Parkflyer conditions with full power at low altitude. Turning at the pylons as close a possible is not as easy as it seems. Concentration and the skills of the Pilot are the decisive points rather than the

Aerobatic models like this will be seen more often in the future.

performance of the motor and I believe that this is much better than a pure material battle. Apart from that, there is a lot of room for experiments within the rules. Maybe a flying wing or a delta is even faster and agile than a conventional design? Park Pylon Racing is meant to be a topic for discussion all the points set out are to be seen as stimulating ideas.

Besides these ideas are also the first models on the market that are designed as real racers with Parkflyer components such as a direct drive Speed 280 and 6 or 7 cells. The models are cut from Styrofoam with real wing sections and a wingspan of about 70 cm. These models look like shrunk Speed 400 racers and are really getting fast and a lot of fun. Yet they are not all that easy to fly as they are small and difficult to see at longer distances. They also need more room to fly than a regular Parkflyer. Finally the increased speed causes a higher potential danger and the flight location should be selected with special care.

CONCLUSIONS

Looking Forward and Looking Back

In every part of our model flying hobby people start thinking after a while, whether all possibilities have been tried and all ideas have been realised still hoping to find new opportunities and challenges.

According to my opinion, Parkflyers are still at the beginning of the process. The radio equipment has reached dimension where a further reduction is not absolutely required any more. But there is a lot to do on the battery side. The NiMh batteries in use have reduced the weight of the models and increased the flight times but new Lithium-Ion or Lithium Polymer batteries will push the limits forward again.

In addition to that, new motors with significantly better efficiency are in the pipeline. Brushless motors suitable for Parkflyers are only at the start of their development. They are interesting in all models where a lot of power is required. The Simprop Extra 330S will soon be able to climb vertically and the torque-roll of the big freestyle aerobatic models is not too far away.

Another trend will be in the field of scale models. There are more than enough interesting originals available and many modellers put more and more building time into their Parkflyers. This what the scale models really deserve. Who says that Parkflyers are throw-away-models?

Furthermore, there seems to be a tendency to bigger and heavier models for Parkflying that are able to cope with the sometimes inevitable wind. Aerobatics will definitely play a bigger role too, as there will be more and more models available that can perform aerobatics and the motors and batteries will be able to supply more power.

On the other hand the days of the only purpose built design are numbered although the fun in flying will remain the focus of the interest.

There is no doubt at all, it will be very interesting to see, what comes up next.

The last words of this book though are reserved for those I have to give my thanks to, as writing this book would not have been possible without them. First of all there is my wife. Several times I have had to persuade her to venture out in the cold of winter to take the in-flight photos as I am still not able to control a model and take a picture at the same time. I have to thank her for her patience, when things were not always going the way they should. The same applies to my children. It is not always a pleasure to be used as a model for pictures but they did their job very well.

Another "thank you very much" goes to my club mates. In the 12 months during which this book was written there were many discussions with a lot of input from them about what to do which way. Their experiences and their advice are also used in this book as one person alone is not able to build and fly as much as necessary. In these months several planes had to be built and the author alone performed more than 500 battery charges as it is my strong opinion that theory is nothing and practical experience finally is the point that counts.

Now, that all photos have been shot and the writing is more or less done so that the manuscript is ready to be sent to the publishers a lot of pictures of the good and the bad flights as well as the curious events during flight testing cross my mind.

It is these experiences and memories, that make our hobby so unique and so satisfying. The Parkflyers with their possibilities of flying at many places surely have taken my heart and I am sure with the possibilities showing up at the horizon they will continue to be my focus for a long time.

I hope, a bit of my enthusiasm has been transmitted to the reader and the Parkflyer virus will grow in you steadily making sure that this interesting section of model flying will spread out more and more. Nevertheless there is still every reason to fly other types of models too, when the opportunity is there!

Hinrik Schulte - March 2005

Useful Addresses

British Model Flying Association (BMFA)

Chacksfield House
31, St. Andrews Road
Leicester
LE2 8RE
01162 440028

www.bmfa.org

The BMFA is the UK national governing body for aeromodelling. Membership includes 3rd party public liability insurance cover. BMFA maintain an extensive list of affiliated clubs.

British Electric Flight Association (BEFA)

www.befa.org

Very informative website with membership application details. Membership benefits include magazine, product sources and reviews, beginners guidance, event reportsd and weather forecasts.